50 city stories explored

ARUP

Foreword
Gregory Hodkinson

The urbanisation challenge is big, it is real and it is with us now. Between 1950 and 2050, the global population is likely to quadruple, from 2.5bn to nearly 10bn. Not so long ago, many commentators believed that such a number would be unsupportable. Yet the inexorable growth continues.

The urban population is growing at an even faster rate. In the next 35 years, the number of city dwellers will increase from 4bn today to over 6.5bn. Africa and Asia will accommodate 90% of this growth.

The rate, scale and concentration of urbanisation in this century is, of course, unprecedented. To accommodate it, the resources of cities, nations, international institutions, civil society and the private sector are being stretched.

If our cities are to be efficient, liveable, resilient and sustainable, the relatively long life-cycle of urban development means we can ill afford to get it wrong. It is a challenge that cities around the world must confront, regardless of their size, wealth or location. Future generations will live with how we handle it. At Arup, we have joined this challenge – with interventions large and small – to deliver better cities in our ongoing mission to shape a better world.

Gregory Hodkinson
Arup Group Chairman

Preface

Cities are inextricably linked to the development of society. As societies change, so do cities, but at no time in human history has the pace of change been so rapid. Over the past 30 years, a radical transformation has taken place, with many existing cities reinventing themselves and new ones emerging almost fully formed.

At Arup, we have witnessed this transformation first-hand and have played an active role in shaping urban environments in positive and far-reaching ways. In cities such as Shanghai, that transformation is obvious to see, with a skyline and footprint that have changed beyond all recognition in little more than a generation.

But other cities have also changed in less visible but no less profound ways. Their needs have changed – including those of the people who live and work in them – and as a result, these cities need to continually update themselves.

Cities still require the core infrastructure that allows people to dwell together – water, waste, transport, energy and communications – but that infrastructure needs to be more flexible, better planned and more efficient. It also needs to be more adaptable, allowing it to change to fit the future needs of cities and city dwellers.

Put simply, good city infrastructure must have a benefit that reaches beyond its immediate intended purpose. It must be meaningful infrastructure.

The old and the new
New infrastructure can be designed to be meaningful from the start, as in Melbourne, where we have helped to create a 50-year plan that allows city administrators to prioritise their long-term investments in line with anticipated population growth.

Hybrid infrastructure projects are meaningful when their benefits extend beyond their immediate primary purpose. Crossrail in London has been designed to bring many different benefits. One new Crossrail station, Canary Wharf, could equally be described as a retail destination or leisure space.

Existing infrastructure becomes meaningful when it can be repurposed to meet new needs, like the Forth Replacement Crossing in Scotland. By rethinking how the existing road bridge and approach roads could be reused, the design of the new replacement crossing has been optimised, reducing materials and costs.

Demands and contradictions

The demands placed upon today's urban environments are often contradictory and are constantly evolving. Cities are increasingly complex – and therefore impossible to fully understand or manage – so they and their communities must be resilient to both day-to-day stresses and unpredictable changes.

Christchurch, New Zealand, was devastated by an earthquake in 2011, but the city is now taking the opportunity to rebuild in a 'smart' way. This means putting in place the ICT infrastructure needed to engage with its citizens, but also boosting the economy by building expertise in data and information services.

One of the most fundamental responses to this resilience challenge is the framework we have created for The Rockefeller Foundation. This allows cities to measure and analyse their own resilience and take practical steps to improve it.

We are also working with organisations such as the C40, whose founding principle is to gather best practice from like-minded cities around the world. By trying to understand the issues and priorities – and learning from the responses of city administrations to foreseen and unforeseen events – a body of knowledge can be created that helps cities to adopt constantly evolving best practice.

>

Birth of a megacity: Shanghai, China
Pages 124 to 133

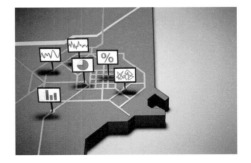

A smart city in action: Sensing City, Christchurch, New Zealand
Pages 40 to 41

Making work safer: Bangladesh
Page 70 to 72

An issue of identity

Cities still face challenges that are specific to their location and to the people who live there. Best practice from around the world can be tailored, but one of the most effective ways of ensuring an authentic and appropriate response is to engage with the people who know their cities the best: the residents.

Working with citizens should be part of any process of change. Cities and their inhabitants need to learn and develop together. The community-led reconstruction programme that followed Hurricane Sandy in New York, for example, shows how important it is to engage with residents to make meaningful improvements and ensure the long-term resilience of the affected communities.

The challenge remains, however: contemporary cities face such a broad range of issues that they cannot possibly be addressed at the same time and in the same way. It therefore becomes important for cities to prioritise in a strategic way – although it's arguably even more important that cities just do something.

Whether it's responses to social unrest, as in London's Tottenham, or urban tragedy, as in Bangladesh, cities must take positive steps to evolve and improve quality of life. Interventions do not have to be large in scale to make an impact. Dashilar in Beijing, for example, is using simple urban furniture to cut down traffic and make city streets safer.

But as the projects contained in this book show, cities have the opportunity to make many interventions for improvement, becoming more 'green', 'intelligent', 'beautiful', 'future facing', 'responsible' and 'resilient'. These themes inform our discussions within this book and in our work with clients around the world.

Fundamentally, the success of any city is based upon the way people respond and interact with it and with each other. Cities may well be complex and constantly changing, but while they remain places where people want to live, work and invest their personal and social capital, they will continue to be successful.

Green

www.arup.com/designbook

A vision to
change a skyline

Beautiful projects can often take a back seat to 'essential' pieces of design, engineering or infrastructure. Persuading governments, local councils, communities and investors to engage with a vision like Thomas Heatherwick's Garden Bridge can be tricky.

The vision is a public garden spanning London's River Thames that will be planted with flowers and trees.

To help people understand exactly what is proposed and what it will look like when built, we created a series of 50 detailed visualisations. Through video, imagery   >

Previous page: Triptych to show visualisation of the evolution of the Garden Bridge.
Opposite: Visualisation on the Garden Bridge

and 3D rendering, we modelled every tree, leaf and flower that will make up the new garden.

And we didn't stop there. We used a garden shed to bring the bridge to life. Inside the shed, people wear virtual-reality goggles to see what the project will look like when complete.

They can smell the vegetation and hear birds tweeting and the noise of London in the background. The result is truly four seasons in one day: it takes in views of and from the bridge and the maturing of plants over 25 years and in different seasons.

It's a vision of the future. And it has helped to convince planners of the value of creating London's first garden over the river.

Project name: The Garden Bridge
Designed for: The Garden Bridge Trust; Transport for London
Designed with: Heatherwick Studio

The Garden Bridge will span the Thames from Temple station to the Southbank Centre, London

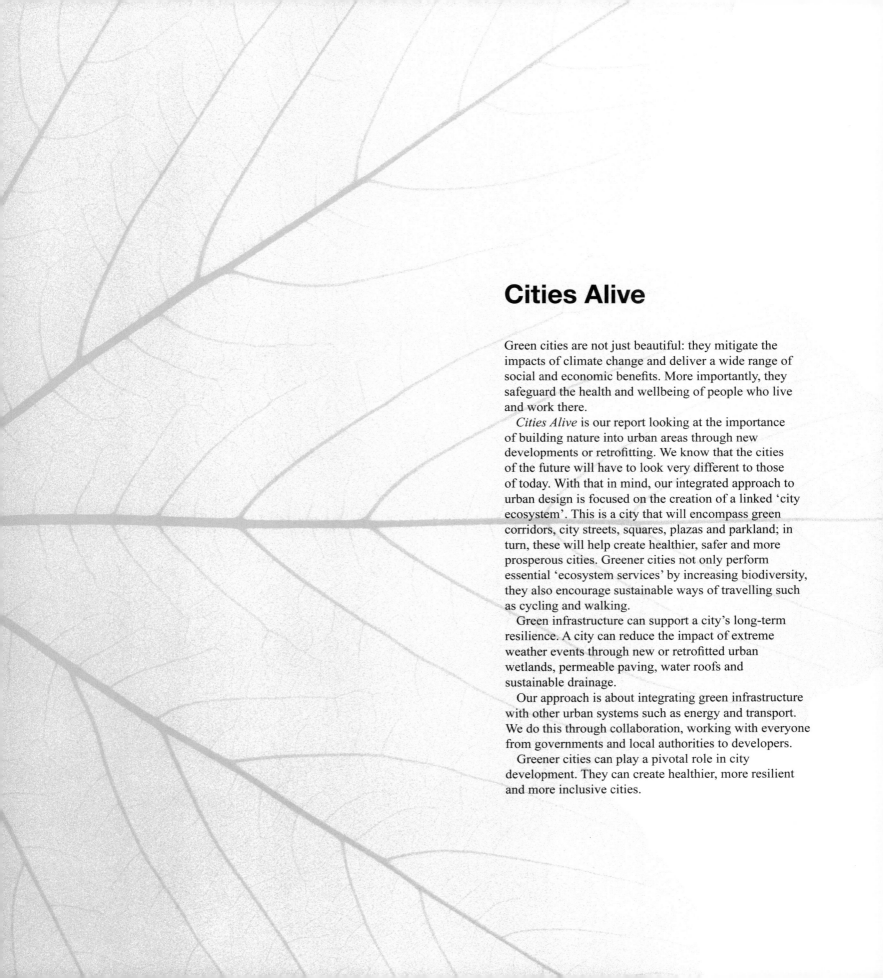

Cities Alive

Green cities are not just beautiful: they mitigate the impacts of climate change and deliver a wide range of social and economic benefits. More importantly, they safeguard the health and wellbeing of people who live and work there.

Cities Alive is our report looking at the importance of building nature into urban areas through new developments or retrofitting. We know that the cities of the future will have to look very different to those of today. With that in mind, our integrated approach to urban design is focused on the creation of a linked 'city ecosystem'. This is a city that will encompass green corridors, city streets, squares, plazas and parkland; in turn, these will help create healthier, safer and more prosperous cities. Greener cities not only perform essential 'ecosystem services' by increasing biodiversity, they also encourage sustainable ways of travelling such as cycling and walking.

Green infrastructure can support a city's long-term resilience. A city can reduce the impact of extreme weather events through new or retrofitted urban wetlands, permeable paving, water roofs and sustainable drainage.

Our approach is about integrating green infrastructure with other urban systems such as energy and transport. We do this through collaboration, working with everyone from governments and local authorities to developers.

Greener cities can play a pivotal role in city development. They can create healthier, more resilient and more inclusive cities.

The sky's the limit

Can a forest be vertical? In the heart of an historic area of Milan, we've used our structural know-how to prove it can. More than 900 cherry, olive and oak trees and other plants have been planted up the exterior of the two 110m and 76m Bosco Verticale buildings.

We tested different tree varieties in wind tunnels to discover how growing them at height would affect the buildings' structures.

Once the trees were planted, some 1,200 ladybirds were released to help improve the site's ecosystem. Today, as residents go about their daily lives inside, the flourishing trees help improve air quality, provide shade and reduce noise pollution.

We've used engineering to help architecture and nature work together. The result is a forest in the air that is as beautiful as it is practical.

Project name: Bosco Verticale
Designed for: Hines Italia SGR SpA
Designed with: Stefano Boeri Architetti;
Barreca & La Varra

After the Games

Olympic success requires careful planning, sheer hard work and dedication. So too did the successful creation of a park when the flame went out on the 2012 London Olympic Games.

The Queen Elizabeth Olympic Park is the culmination of a complex design journey. Our immense knowledge of the site meant that we were the key consultants in the extraordinary task of removing the Olympic footprint and preparing and designing the park in its legacy form. Working as part of a multi-consultant team, we played a key role in delivering the detailed design for the South Park. We undertook a complex coordination process to ensure that all parts of the design worked together.

Below the working surface of the park lies a dense underground landscape of utility runs, in different ground conditions and levels. The park design at surface had to be carefully fashioned within this challenging post-industrial site.

As well as coordinating the work of the consultant teams, we worked with other major park projects such as the Olympic Stadium, the ArcelorMittal Orbit and the Aquatics Centre.

Europe's largest new park for a century has already welcomed more than 4.5m visitors since reopening. It's a lasting legacy, born of dedication and hard work, for Londoners and visitors to enjoy.

Project name: London 2012 Olympic and Paralympic Games South Park; London 2012 Olympic and Paralympic Post Games Transformation; Queen Elizabeth Olympic Park – South Park Plaza
Designed for: Olympic Delivery Authority; London Legacy Development Corporation
Designed with: LDA Design; Hargreaves Associates; James Corner Field Operations; Make Architects; Atkins; Allies & Morrison

What is your favorite part of our new home?

my favorite part is every part.

A sustainable education

An empty car park in the middle of downtown Newark, New Jersey might seem an unlikely setting for a 'middle-income utopia'. But all the collaborators on this plan shared the common ambition of transforming a neighbourhood. And we've made it a reality.

The mixed-use development project is a new community of homes, shops and business spaces with education at its heart. The vision includes more than 9,000m^2 of educational facilities, 200 apartments – some of which will be homes for teachers – 1,300m^2 of childcare facilities and more than 6,000m^2 of retail space. We hope that the educational centre will act as a vibrant hub for the community, driving regeneration over the longer term without forcing residents out.

Limited by a tight budget, we fostered enthusiastic support from state and city government and developed inexpensive and efficient solutions. Take the school façades. They feature a mixture of brick and glazing that is economical and complements the surrounding architecture. We also championed Newark's first green street, where stormwater is recycled to water the trees and plants.

Affordable regeneration is an ambitious vision. However, this project shows how architecture, planning and engineering can contribute to social improvement agendas – without costing the earth.

Project name: Teachers Village, Newark
Designed for: RBH Group
Designed with: Richard Meier & Partners Architects LLP; KSS Architects

Name Sanai Chatman

Draw a picture of you in SPARK's new home.

What is your favorite part of our new home?

I love the school you made. My favorite one is the playground.

The littlest local residents have shared their appreciation of their new community by way of crayon artwork

Pointing the way ahead

Hunter's Point South enjoys magnificent views of the Manhattan skyline. During its 200-year urban history, it has had several incarnations. Once an industrial hub, with warehouses, factories and a ferry terminal, more recently it had fallen into disrepair.

This semi-derelict site – on a prime waterside area in New York – offered great opportunities for regeneration and redevelopment. Importantly, the space also had the potential to become a new shared hub, building community spirit.

Ahead of the new development – with responsibility for the infrastructure and the park – we began an extensive consultation with stakeholders. The community was actively involved in telling us what would make a real difference to their lives.

We then combined the City of New York's masterplan with local input to develop designs that transformed the once underused site >

into a large waterfront park – complete with a dog run – and 1,040m of new streets and bike-ways. All of this will accommodate the current and future development of residential housing.

Our initiatives also include a continuous planting zone and porous pavements, meaning they're less susceptible to flooding and will encourage tree growth. Meanwhile, the landscape of the streets and the park incorporates measures that reduce both stormwater flooding and water pollution.

The park has breathed new life into the area. These days, it's regularly used for events of all kinds, from beach volleyball to silent discos and movie nights. When the new mixed-use neighbourhood is completed, it will deliver a brand-new and affordable community, the largest of its kind to be built in New York since the 1970s.

Project name: Hunter's Point South
Designed for: New York City Economic Development Corporation
Designed with: Thomas Balsley Associates; Weiss/Manfredi; CH2M HILL; Yu & Associates; B-A Engineering PC; Great Ecology; AG Consulting Engineering PC; VJ Associates; AKRF, Inc; Naik Consulting Group PC; Siteworks

35% less
electricity than
traditional
air-cooled air
conditioning systems
and…

20% less
than individual
water-cooled air
conditioning systems

Annual savings will be
85m kWh

representing
59,000 tonnes
of CO_2 and
HK$76.5m

Using the sea to go green

Each city's location presents different needs and opportunities. Take Hong Kong. Here, air conditioning accounts for almost 25% of energy use in the commercial area, so it makes sense to try to reduce it.

The Kai Tak Development is surrounded by the ocean, so we developed a district cooling system that uses seawater. Used at this scale – over 2.24m m^2 – for commercial buildings, transport, retail and hotels, the system is much more efficient than when used for single buildings or small groups. It also frees up a lot of space. For example, roofs, which would normally house air conditioning units, can be turned into green space, further improving air quality and cooling this part of the city.

The first of its kind in Hong Kong, this smart system proves that bespoke approaches make a real difference.

Project name: District Cooling System in Kai Tak Development
Designed for: Electrical and Mechanical Services Department,
Hong Kong Special Administrative Region (HKSAR) Government

24

Cutting carbon
the smart way

How do you ensure that a city's most iconic and historic buildings remain efficient? We're helping The Crown Estate to do just that by reducing carbon emissions across its central London portfolio, in keeping with its reputation for sustainable development.

The project hinges on predicting, then validating, the carbon emissions from buildings, which allows The Crown Estate to benchmark and improve performance. It's as much about setting targets for new developments as it is about improving the old.

The impact of our work is already visible: The Crown Estate is working towards an ambitious target of a 50% reduction by 2022.

Running alongside the carbon reduction plan is an ecology masterplan reintroducing nature into the urban environment. This will enhance biodiversity, improve the health of the local environment and contribute to the long-term value and sustainability of the area.

We are planning 1,500m^2 of new green space on rooftops and urban spaces by 2016. This will create new habitats for birds, bees and other insects – and make this corner of central London a better place for its human tenants and visitors too.

Project name: Development Sustainability Principles
framework and ecology masterplan
Designed for: The Crown Estate, London

50%
2022 target for
reduction in carbon
intensity across
the estate

1,500m^2
of new green space
planned for rooftops
and urban spaces
by 2016

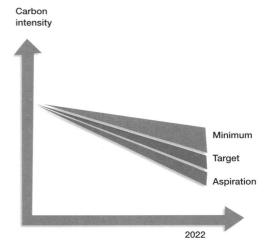

The Crown Estate is committed
to reducing carbon emissions
across its portfolio

Delivering a new shopping experience

Traffic, pollution and noise. When they're reduced, they make cities better places to live, work and visit. We kept this in mind while we worked with The Crown Estate to reduce delivery-vehicle traffic on one of London's busiest shopping roads, Regent Street.

Research showed that some 20% of traffic consisted of delivery vans. This rose to 35% in peak times as uncontrolled deliveries caused significant congestion and road blockages. We launched three initiatives to change store deliveries. First, a logistics facility consolidating shop deliveries has reduced traffic from participating companies by 80%. Second, a preferred-supplier scheme has cut the number of deliveries to offices. And third,

final-mile electric bike delivery allows suppliers to have smaller deliveries made by bike during the day.

It's a win-win approach: shoppers are happier and there are more of them. Shop workers spend less time unpacking ad hoc deliveries. Stock management is easier to control. Perhaps best of all, there are fewer traffic jams, and pollution levels have been cut. That's what we call retail therapy.

Project name: Regent Street Freight Reduction Scheme
Designed for: The Crown Estate, London
Designed with: Clipper Logistics; Gnewt Cargo

Intelligent

www.arup.com/designbook

Travel building blocks

Scandinavian design is revered for its minimalism. So when it came to designing new stations for Cityringen, an extension to the metro system in Copenhagen, we opted for a pared-back design.

The new circle line runs through the city's historic centre and links to the existing metro. It's all about designing in small spaces. We took a modular approach, stitching stations into their environment using the same base elements, customised only where necessary. This minimises disruption and is economical.

Each neighbourhood can modify the core design of its station and incorporate ideas and motifs inspired by the surroundings. This doesn't just strengthen each neighbourhood's identity, it also helps people find their nearest station through inferred wayfinding.

For example, Enghave Plads station features brown bricks to proudly reflect the style of buildings in the former working-class neighbourhood. København H, the main Copenhagen station, sports bright red panels. This signals that you can transfer from metro to regular red trains. It is also the colour of the old station building.

In a city where people usually prefer to travel above ground by bike or on foot, passengers can now get from the street to the platform without feeling as though they are venturing underground. To achieve this, most of the 17 new stations feature skylights. These provide natural light on the platforms, are energy efficient and help bring the outside in.

Cityringen has set new standards for modern metro systems. It shows that delightful design can be achieved in small spaces. And it proves that major engineering projects can be stylishly minimalist.

Project name: Cityringen, Denmark
Designed for: Metroselskabet I/S
Designed with: COWI A/S; SYSTRA

Left: Design details of the new stations on Copenhagen's Cityringen reflect their locations. Below: A visualisation of one of the Cityringen station platforms

A design for life

Our pared-back approach to station design extended to the 1.5m m² docklands redevelopment in the Nordhavnen area of Copenhagen. At this station, a dual-track metro branches off from the Cityringen subway. The design was inspired by its locality: it is elevated above ground and has an urban aesthetic. Simple shapes and materials echo many of the buildings in this former industrial area.

This is the first in a string of new stations that will link to the rest of the Copenhagen metro system. It sets a benchmark for elevated stations in Copenhagen. Like this shining example, others will have space beneath for play areas and coffee shops, boosting the economic regeneration of the area and improving the experience for passengers.

Project name: Cityringen extension to Nordhavnen
Designed for: Metroselskabet I/S
Designed with: Ramboll AS; COBE Architects A/S

"It's stylish. It's very modern. It feels like the future of New York."

Marcina Alexandre,
Queens Village resident

Transforming transport and urban placemaking

If you want a prosperous city, and one that people want to live in, you have to allow them to get in, out and around the place easily.

With that in mind, one of Manhattan's busiest station interchanges has been transformed. Used by 300,000 people daily, it unites six subway stations and 12 subway lines into one transport hub. It's called the Fulton Center.

Lower Manhattan's response to Grand Central Station is a stunning new hub that allows people to get to their different destinations easily. Essentially, it helps keep New York City moving.

After the destruction of 9/11, there was a need to revitalise this part of Lower Manhattan. We started work with a planning study and kept this context in mind, along with the need to provide connections across the area. Our plan included river-to-river access, subway network benefits and the architecture of the centre.

When it came to the centre itself, we had to first understand the way the station was used. Ramps, hidden entrances, missing staircases and confusing signs led to crowding and pinch-points throughout the station and 'spill out' on to surrounding streets. There was a clear need for better access channels, and more of them.

>

The dome and oculus

Natural light has always played an important role in the New York City subway system. So the creation of the Fulton Center was an opportunity to give passengers better amenities, safety and comfort. The result is seen throughout the transit centre, but it is best shown in the 16m-diameter glass and steel oculus at the top of the dome. This sits on top of the central atrium space, above the entrance and retail pavilion, and draws in natural light. The dome is lined with a cable net – the Sky Reflector-Net – which has almost 1,000 reflective panels that bounce natural light down to even the lowest level of the atrium.

We worked with the architect and artist to understand how factors such as air pressure, interior temperature and building movement would influence the movement of the net. We then developed 815 unique scenarios that each produced a slightly different cable net shape. Finally, we analysed the intensity and distribution of the light that would filter into the space below.

"It's like a whole new transformation, such a unique design. I really like when it's a sunny day and you stand right under the ceiling."

Tasul Islam, Bronx resident

Using our MassMotion software, we developed a model that mapped the movement of more than 48,000 people through the station at any one time – allowing us to test our plans and the project's constructability.

The result is a much improved user experience. There are new direct connections between train lines, wider corridors with daylight flooding in and new mezzanines to separate passengers. This means less crowding, a reduction in loading and unloading delays and improved security.

As well as better signage, the spaces use intuitive wayfinding. Daylight and architectural finishes give passengers open sightlines that help them navigate their routes.

The most obvious symbol of the new Fulton Center is the hub. A huge public space, it enables connections throughout the centre, improves street access and includes retail space. We advised on the inclusion of the planned retail and dining spaces because they improve the passenger experience and support the local area. This will also increase non-farebox revenue opportunities.

Sustainability was an important focus. From the outset, energy efficiency, life-cycle value, pollution prevention and responsible waste management were priorities. Daylight is maximised. Energy usage is reduced. And more than 20% of materials used were sourced locally and made of recycled content.

>

"This is a great station to transfer. It's much easier. You have the trains right here – before, you would get lost. Now it's just very wide and open."

Marquis Burkes, Brooklyn resident

Technology to improve travel

People move through the Fulton Center with ease because it was designed for fluid movement. We created the MassMotion pedestrian simulation software specifically to understand how people would move through the space. The microsimulation software addressed the complex – and unique – spatial characteristics of the Fulton Center, which existing software wasn't able to do. It allowed us to analyse complex interchanges and vertical transitions quickly. It took into account the many interactions passengers have on their journeys, such as when they cross each other's paths and how they reach different parts of the station. And it analysed the cumulative effect of decisions made by individuals, such as choosing to take the stairs or escalators. We identified problems before the design was made real.

"The Corbin Building is very beautiful on the outside. Inside they left all the architectural detail, which is really gorgeous. I take the escalator and just look. It's so beautiful."

Lama Fox, New York resident

The Corbin Building

Blending the very best of old elegance with the convenience of the new has revitalised the landmark Corbin Building. Built in 1889, it had become a blackened relic, earmarked for demolition. But it has now been restored to its former glory. Using 3D laser scanning, we were able to understand how the building was constructed and use this to inform the upgrade. We uncovered techniques such as Guastavino tile structural floor arches, designed for fire resistance and their ability to accommodate load, as well as being quick to construct. Renovations included structural underpinning, using mini-piles that were installed by machine, and hand-dug pits when large machines could not be used in such a confined space. We were then able to refurbish the interior and façade.

The basement and ground floor have been transformed into an entrance to the new Fulton Center. And escalators move through the Corbin Building so visitors can enjoy a piece of New York's past.

The Fulton Center hasn't just transformed the way people travel around the city. It's also having a ripple effect on the surrounding area, making it become a more desirable place to live and work.

Furthermore, it's given this famous area a new urban landmark, helping reshape Lower Manhattan and New York City as a whole.

Project name: Fulton Center
Designed for: MTA Capital Construction; New York City Transit Authority
Designed with: HDR/Daniel Frankfurt; Page Ayres Cowley Architects; Grimshaw Architects; Lee Harris Pomeroy Architects

Edgar Pieterse
Towards a more just city

Q: What does a city mean to you?
A city is inherently complex. I've always been really influenced by the Italian philosopher Italo Calvino. In his wonderful book *Invisible Cities*, he talks about cities as a rebus of desire and fear.

"With cities, it is as with dreams: everything imaginable can be dreamed, but even the most unexpected dream is a rebus that conceals a desire or, its reverse, a fear. Cities, like dreams, are made of desires and fears, even if the thread of their discourse is secret, their rules are absurd, their perspectives deceitful, and everything conceals something else."

A city channels desire for a different future, a different horizon, different possibilities. But at the same time it channels anxiety about the difficulty of attaining that. It generates this incredibly dense and complex and, in some ways, really beautiful atmosphere of competing ideas and agendas.

Q: Why do people want to live and work in cities?
People are drawn to cities because they are a horizon of possibility – but not everyone's desires can be fulfilled. People are drawn to them, but they're also repelled by the harshness of urban life.

Q: How important is sustainability in a city?
Sustainability is not just important – it is non-negotiable. But it is not a straightforward matter, because there are very powerful interests competing around the imperative of sustainability.

Q: What is a 'just city'?
As a global community of nations and of citizens we all acknowledge that everyone is equal and everyone should have their rights fulfilled. That's not just political rights but also the right to shelter, the right to water, the right to the basics of life.

The problem is that cities are profoundly unjust and marked by deep inequalities. The just city is a city where everyone can pursue their rights without the threat of persecution. But there are a worryingly large number of cities where there's no evidence that the political elites are committed to the idea of universal socioeconomic or human rights. This is a phenomenon in the Middle East and in Eastern Asia, but also in very large parts of Africa. We all have a pretty clear idea about what the just city is, but we are a long way from seeing that realised.

Q: What is the single most important challenge for a city?
The most important challenge for any city is to embrace diversity. It is to understand that by its very nature a city is an agglomeration of multiple histories, multiple types, different languages, different cultures, different ways of being in the world. Finding ways to facilitate diversity is what makes a city comfortable in its own skin. It also gives access to the largest pool of resources for creativity and innovation. If a city is able to tap into that, it can marshal the various groups and interests and deal with larger questions around areas such as sustainability or social justice.

Q: How important is it for cities to share knowledge?
In many ways, cities everywhere, whether they're in the rich OECD world or in the developing world, face similar problems. They have got to grapple with the question of transforming their economies so that they become more resource-efficient and less wasteful in terms of emissions. They've got to attend to the fact that the people who live in the city need access to jobs. They've got to ensure that their population can access basic services like health and education, so they can enter the economy in a productive sense. The nature and the scale and the complexity of these imperatives of urban development apply as much in Spain where you've got 25%–30% youth unemployment as it does in Cape Town where you've got 30%–40% unemployment.

Q: What makes a city great?
A city that is marked by a dynamic and diverse art scene has in some ways solved one of the biggest questions: how do you create a cultural environment wherein the most complicated and fearless people are able to articulate what the society is about? That, for me, is the sign of an amazing city.

Giving the arts free rein makes any city great. If you have a dense milieu of artistic production, you automatically have all the other elements of innovation that can produce fantastic artefacts in the urban realm. The core for me is political tolerance of free artistic expression. If that's in evidence, the other things we associate with great cities, like fine architecture or amazing cuisine, would also probably be in evidence.

Q: Are we living through a complicated time for cities?
We're talking about finding ways to propel the growth of cities, to build in a new way, to live differently in the next 10, 20 or 30 years – or else as a civilisation we're stuffed. The stakes have never been this high. We live in a more complex time than ever before.

Edgar Pieterse is a scholar and writer. He holds the South African Research Chair in Urban Policy at the University of Cape Town and is director of the African Centre for Cities.

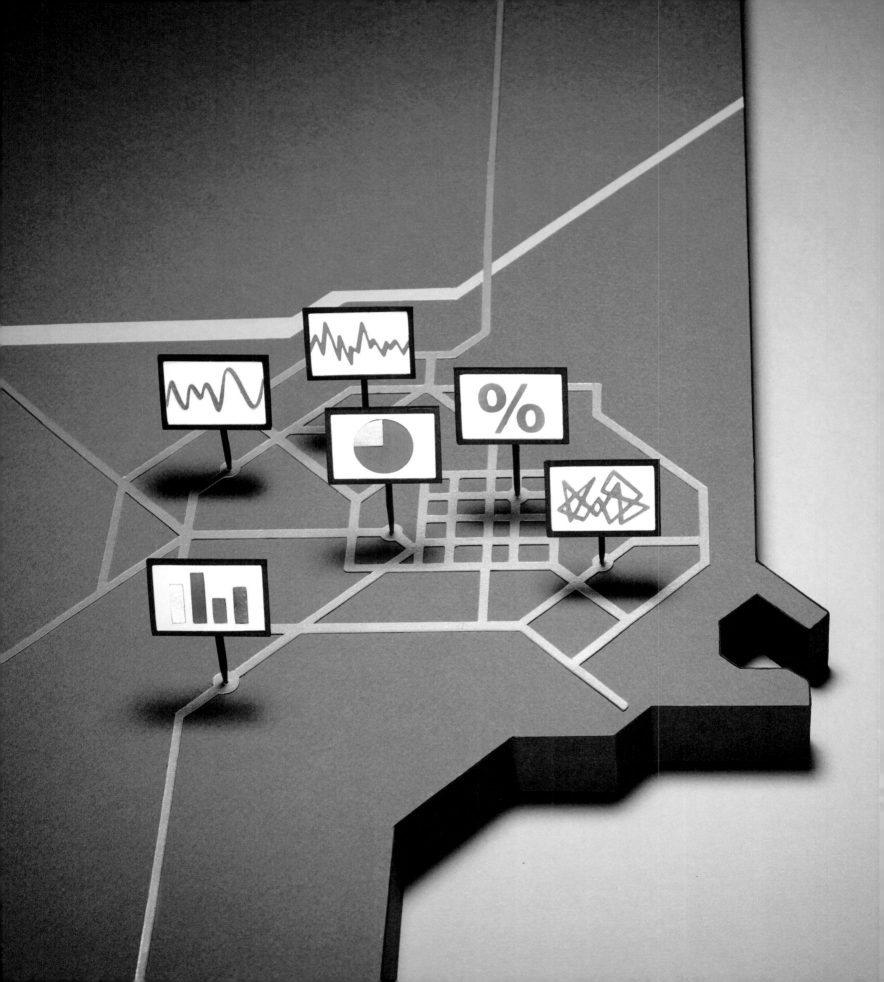

A smart city in action

Adversity can present opportunity. That was certainly true in the aftermath of the 2011 Christchurch earthquake in New Zealand. The process of rebuilding the city presented a unique chance to include sensors in its infrastructure, with the aim of creating a 21st-century living lab that can test ideas many other cities want to develop.

We created a digital masterplan to advise how to establish this 'Sensing City', which would pioneer the use of information to manage urban living. A key aim is to use real-time data to show how cities really work, rather than looking at patterns in retrospect. Crucially, the initiative has also set out to develop a data platform for residents to contribute data about things that matter to them, rather than waiting for regulators to tell them.

We also advised on the creation of data services to position Christchurch as a world leader in information marketplaces. This will encourage investment and boost the economy.

A world first, Sensing City will position Christchurch at the forefront of the smart technology revolution.

Project name: Sensing City
Designed for: Infratil Limited

Breathe again

In a study about how air quality affects respiratory illness, data will be gathered about medication used to control lung disease. In addition, air quality will be monitored. Christchurch will be the first place in the world where people can see the link between air pollution and respiratory illness. It's about creating a body of research and improving lives in the city.

That's how the light gets in

Priceless works by artists such as Rembrandt, Van Gogh and Vermeer are housed in the Rijksmuseum. It is the cultural calling card of the Netherlands and attracts more than a million visitors every year. A ten-year renovation has restored the museum to its former glory.

The museum had suffered generations of adaptations that wore away much of its charm. In some cases, internal frescoes had been painted over and ceilings lowered. We reinstated its original design while bringing it up to 21st-century standards.

We reinstated and connected the original atria to create a light, open space that connects the two halves of the building. Daylight and state-of-the-art electric lighting in the galleries illuminate the restored frescoes, 19th-century detailing and, importantly, the art.

Invisible installations give visitors a better experience of the art: integrated air conditioning and new insulation technology protect the artworks. They do this without changing the geometry of the building and while retaining full flexibility for the art displays. The building's energy system has also been brought up to date.

Today, this historic yet modern museum is a joy to visit. It's the perfect environment for enjoying art.

Project name: Rijksmuseum, Amsterdam
Designed for: Programmadirectie Het Nieuwe Rijksmuseum (HNR)
Designed with: Cruz y Ortiz Architects

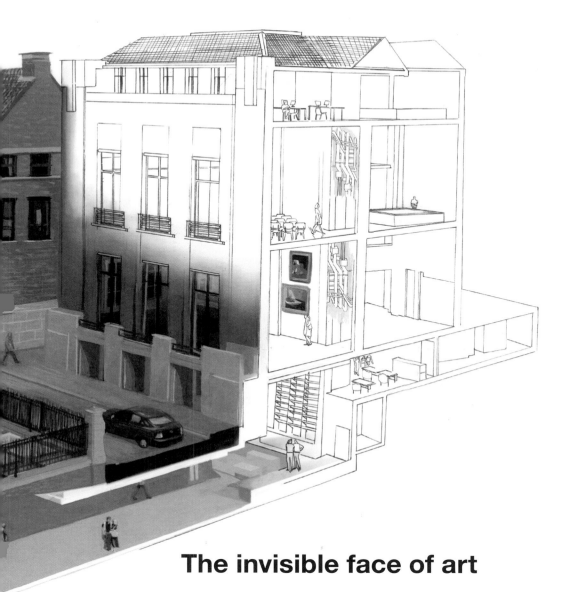

The invisible face of art

The Mauritshuis in the Hague is home to the very best Dutch Golden Age paintings, including Vermeer's *Girl with a Pearl Earring*. So, when it underwent a two-year renovation, making sure the art was seen in the best possible light was an absolute priority.

An extension to connect the Mauritshuis with the Society de Witte building opposite, now the Royal Dutch Shell Wing, doubled the size of the 17th-century city palace. The Mauritshuis's existing two-storey basement – which contained a nuclear bunker to protect the art – was partly demolished and extended underneath the street to link with the new wing. Visitors now enter the museum through the light-filled foyer created by connecting the two buildings.

Our design team subtly incorporated changes into the existing gallery and the new wing, ensuring the visitors'

focus remains on the art collection, while fire safety and security devices work behind the scenes. Using digital and 3D models, we were able to map and understand the existing structure, then hide new technology such as temperature and humidity sensors behind the wall covering.

The result is an almost invisible facelift that protects the museum's priceless collection, ensures visitors have a better experience and enhances the beautiful buildings. Most importantly, it provides a safe, modern home for some of the world's greatest masterpieces.

Project name: Mauritshuis
Designed for: Stichting Koninklijk Kabinet van Schilderijen Mauritshuis
Designed with: Hans van Heeswijk Architecten

A talking transport system

Technology can revitalise transport networks. In the Irish city of Limerick, increased traffic threatened to worsen the congestion already caused by poor traffic signal coordination, street parking and freight loading. This didn't just make buses run late, it also affected the prosperity of the entire city.

Our study revealed that simply linking up the traffic signal network would lead to a smarter system.

So we got them talking. We linked the traffic lights to a central system so they could respond to fluctuations in traffic and quickly produce fault alerts if one set wasn't working. Sensors were installed to differentiate between regular vehicles and buses, giving buses priority at traffic lights. Old-fashioned parking discs were put to work alongside smartphone apps. Electronic signs help motorists find empty parking spaces. Even before you reach the city, electronic signs advise about routes and parking and in wet conditions warn against potential flooding.

Congestion has reduced and public transport is more widely used and reliable. Limerick is on the move again.

Project name: Limerick City Smart Mobility
Designed for: Limerick City and County Council

Wood is good

Wood has been an important construction material since building began. Today, it is enjoying a revival. The advantages for the construction industry are clear: wood can enable better, faster and cheaper construction for commercial and residential buildings.

The wood that is able to meet this demand is modern-engineered; products are a world away from lightweight timber-frame buildings, and include cross-laminated timber and glue-laminated timber. These products allow engineers, designers and architects to use wood in ways that were not previously possible.

Tall, strong buildings can be constructed quickly off-site, and assembled on-site in small spaces.

Wood offers another advantage: it is sustainable. It is the only completely renewable building material. It has no embodied energy because it is grown with solar power.

Advances in engineering mean that even issues such as poor acoustics in wooden builds (traditionally solved by the inclusion of concrete floors) and fire engineering (more often a perceived threat rather than a reality) are being addressed.

Using wood isn't the answer for every building. But it is increasing its share of the market. And that doesn't have to come at the high price of deforestation. The forests of North America alone grow enough wood for a new 20-storey building every 13 minutes – and that's a lot of timber.

Wood can be tall...

It might be one of the oldest and most traditional building materials, but wood is back at the heart of innovation. Timber is no longer associated only with low and mid-rise buildings. In Dornbirn, Austria, we researched and then built an eight-storey wooden prototype.

We have also co-funded further research looking at whether we could build a 40-storey timber high-rise. And we are now working on plans for a 20-storey timber building, also in Austria.

Wood comes with challenges, especially in terms of fire engineering and acoustics. However, by combining it with concrete slabs, we can deal with both. It takes our specialist expertise to demonstrate that using timber with other materials can unlock the potential of wood for the construction industry. For example, when the LifeCycle Tower is built, a concrete evacuation route will replace the need for a sprinkler system.

We are forecasting a lower carbon footprint, combined with ease of reuse at the end of the building's life. It's yet more proof that wood is good.

Project name: LifeCycle Tower Research; SuperBioMarkt; LCT ONE
Designed for: Cree
Designed with: Cree; Council on Tall Buildings and Urban Habitat

...and sustainable

Wood is not just good. It's also green. Sky asked us to create an educational facility for its campus in west London that would provide training for staff, graduates and apprentices. The brief also called for spaces for community engagement with schoolchildren – and for a sustainable building.

Wood was the answer. Not only is it a sympathetic building material, it also has a low carbon footprint.

We used cost-effective, modular timber panels, which are flexible enough to adapt to different configurations. One of the largest timber buildings of its kind, the four-storey structure and envelope took just eight weeks to build. It was made off-site and assembled on-site. This ensured a speedy and safer build and further reduced the carbon footprint. The exposed wood structure makes it not just a sustainable showcase, but a warm, inspiring and unusual building.

Project name: Sky Believe in Better Building
Designed for: Sky

Right: Endless Stair, shown outside Tate Modern in London, is now on the move. Left: Endless Stair in Milan

When wood and art meet

Endless Stair is an installation with a difference: a work of art that is also a research project.

Originally installed outside Tate Modern in London, its prefabricated, perpendicular layers were put together on-site just eight months after the idea was first conceived.

This arresting sculpture's interlocking staircases are made of cross-laminated American tulipwood panels. We tested the material to ensure the Escher-like structure would not only be beautiful to look at, but also robust enough for people to walk on. The innovative use of cross-laminated hardwood timber ensured that the panels used in the sculpture remained slim and elegant.

Tulipwood, one of the world's most sustainable building materials, is rare in projects of this type. Endless Stair demonstrates the possible new uses of this old material, which are, like the installation itself, well and truly endless.

Project name: Endless Stair
Designed for: The London Design Festival
(supported by the American Hardwood Export Council)
Designed with: dRMM Architects

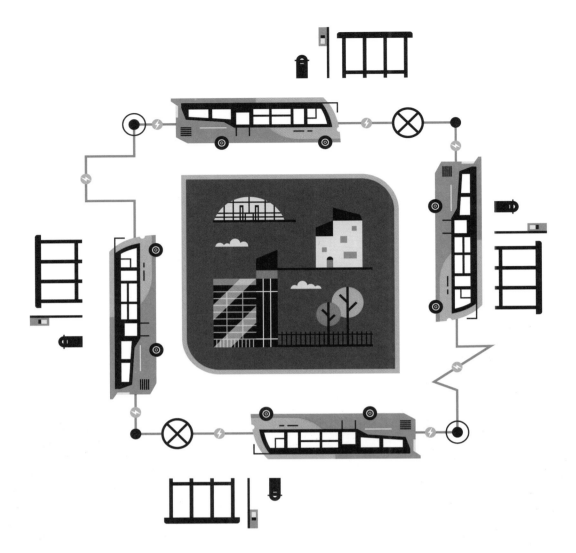

Keeping the wheels turning

Pioneers don't always end up with arrows in their backs. In Milton Keynes, we set up a joint venture to run a fleet of electric buses using wireless-charging technology, and it's a sound investment. We believed the system would work, so we built it for real.

Standard battery-powered electric buses require batteries so huge that they're impractical. The solution is wireless charging. This means the batteries are continuously topped up during the day, giving the buses the same range as diesel models.

Running wireless buses on this one route is removing 270 tonnes of carbon from the atmosphere every year. We've proved it works, so other cities are now keen to use the technology. And that makes Milton Keynes a pioneer.

Project name: Route 7 electric bus demonstration programme
Designed for: Milton Keynes Council; Arriva
Designed with: MBK Arup Sustainable Projects Ltd; Mitsui & Co Europe Plc; eFleet Integrated Service Ltd; Milton Keynes Council; Arriva; Wrightbus Limited; IPT Technology; Chargemaster Plc; SSE; Western Power Distribution

Responsible

www.arup.com/designbook

The Crossrail challenge

Swanlea
School

"We spent a lot of time explaining the rhythms of the school... They aren't organisations that can quickly change. We haven't had disruption to public exams and we haven't had issues around noise."

Brenda Landers, head teacher, Swanlea School

Can you tunnel through the heart of one of the world's biggest cities without interrupting day-to-day life? That was the challenge we embraced when the Crossrail project got under way in London.

Construction projects don't come much bigger than Crossrail, a 118km railway line passing under London. The central part of the line comprises two 21km tunnels that will connect passengers with existing rail and underground lines.

Tunnelling on this scale has the potential to cause significant problems to the existing buildings above. So, we assessed the impact of tunnelling on 17,000

structures along the route, as well as on underground utilities and London Underground lines.

We adapted the technology used to monitor massive amounts of Formula 1 racing car data to devise a system to monitor building subsidence. It acts as an early warning system, so we can respond quickly to protect buildings against damage when necessary.

For the businesses and homes above the tunnels, the measure of our success comes in the continuation of life and work as usual.

Swanlea School sits partially on top of Whitechapel station, which is 20m below ground. This proved to be

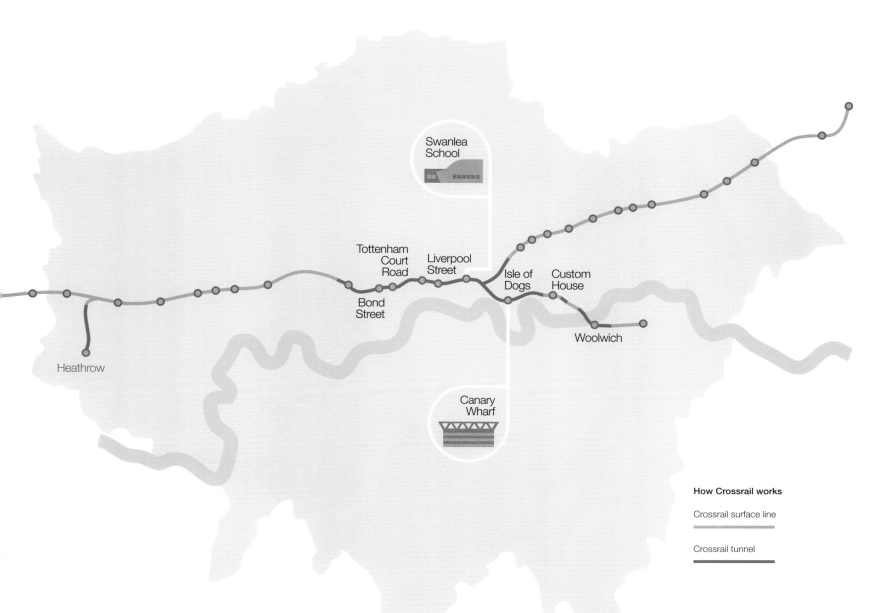

Swanlea
School

Tottenham
Court
Road

Liverpool
Street

Bond
Street

Isle of
Dogs

Custom
House

Heathrow

Woolwich

Canary
Wharf

How Crossrail works

━━━ Crossrail surface line

━━━ Crossrail tunnel

Rail to change a city

Crossrail is currently Europe's biggest civil engineering project. It will create an east–west high frequency rail line in London and significantly reduce journey times to many destinations. Up to 24 trains will travel in each direction every hour through the central underground section.

Ten new stations are being built, eight of them below ground and integrated with the existing London Underground and Docklands Light Railway. The stations have been designed for much larger passenger numbers than any London Underground station. Platforms are 200m long and each train will carry up to 1,500 people. The most intensive construction effort is centred on the two 21km tunnels under the centre of the city.

"We have had concerts all the time. And the prom was able to go on."

Brenda Landers, head teacher, Swanlea School

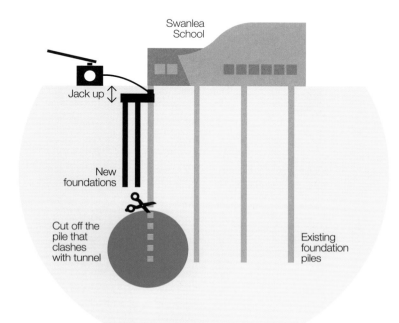

Swanlea
School

Jack up ↕

The piles under the school
could be jacked up if the
building started to move

New
foundations

Cut off the
pile that
clashes
with tunnel

Existing
foundation
piles

one of our biggest challenges. The school is supported by concrete piles in the ground. Unfortunately, these were in the way of the eastbound platform tunnel. After devising a way of cutting the piles underground, we needed to support the school building.

Our solution was the installation of six mini-piles with a pair of jacks around each one that connected directly to the school building. This was in turn covered with sophisticated monitoring equipment to check for any movement to within a millimetre or two. If the building started to move, it could be jacked up again. The technology that underpinned our ability to monitor and interpret data gave us valuable information about how Swanlea and other buildings on the Crossrail route would act. That means no school – or work – days have been missed.

Project name: Crossrail
Designed for: Crossrail Ltd
Designed with: Atkins

What lies beneath

Canary
Wharf

100,000m³
dock water pumped out

135,000m³
soil excavated

Built in the middle of an existing ship dock, Crossrail's Canary Wharf station will better connect the financial district in the east of the city with the West End, the City of London and Heathrow.

Finding a suitable location for the new rail station was an early challenge. It got even trickier when the answer came in the shape of part of a dock.

This meant designing a 60,000m² building that would be surrounded by water. Our team helped to design a fully submerged station with shops, restaurants and a new public garden above the waterline.

From the outside, people will see a ship-like structure topped with one of the world's largest continuous timber roofs. This new station is surrounded by some of London's most valuable properties, so planning approvals required that the construction didn't disrupt residents, which include four major bank headquarters.

A silent piling system was used to minimise noise during construction. Innovative interlocking joints then created a watertight perimeter wall. With this in place, the dock water was drained out before the station was built inside the walls.

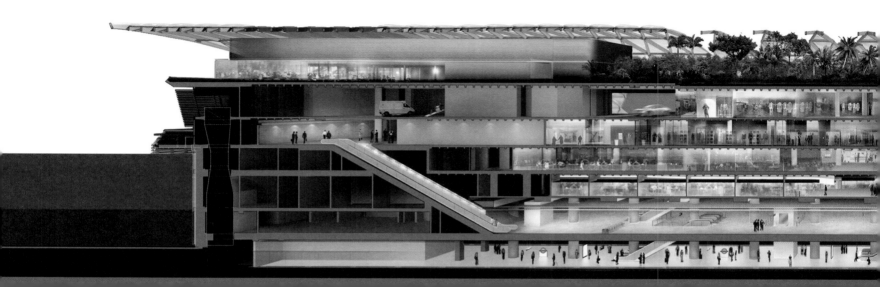

One of the station's invisible strengths is that it is the ultimate flexible space. For example, if the retail levels are no longer needed three decades from now, they can be removed completely and the station will remain fully functional. Or, if the retail area needs to be overhauled, it can easily be reconfigured. Substantial changes can be made to the size, shape and height of the units, including the creation of new atria or layouts, without any structural obstacles.

While the Crossrail station itself is virtually complete, trains won't start running until 2018. Despite the complex construction, the project was delivered early and under budget.

We went beyond the functional brief to deliver something beautiful and flexible. The result enhances the value of a transport node that will improve the connectivity and desirability of Canary Wharf as a place to live and work.

Project name: Canary Wharf Crossrail Station
Designed for: Canary Wharf Contractors Ltd
Designed with: Foster + Partners; Adamson Associates International; Tony Meadows Associates

On top of the station is a
310m
continuous timber roof, curved like an arch

Under the timber roof is a
3,500m²
garden...

...below this are
four
floors of flexible retail, leisure and restaurant space

A FUTURE MODEL CITY BASED ON 'SMART, GREEN AND RESILIENT' PRINCIPLES

ADVISORY ON DEVELOPMENT, MASTERPLANNING, URBAN DESIGN, SUSTAINABILITY, LANDSCAPE,

Flying high

Great planning and project management are the foundation of Taoyuan Aerotropolis, a new extension at Taiwan Taoyuan International Airport. This smart, green and resilient project will eventually cover 6,850ha of land. It will include civic space and homes, plus specific areas driving economic growth. There will be an enterprise zone for R&D firms and start-ups, a free trade zone with links to the existing seaport, and a zone for exhibitions, conferences, short-term stays and entertainment.

Years spent advising on cities helped us to develop a masterplan to ensure that the new rail system integrated well with external networks and promoted the Aerotropolis and its benefits to the public.

We also recommended irrigation ponds to help reduce flooding, multiple public spaces and carbon-neutral housing. When complete, the Aerotropolis will create an estimated NT$2,300bn in economic revenue.

Project name: Taoyuan Aerotropolis
Designed for: Taoyuan County Government

CREATION OF UP TO 300,000 JOBS

ECONOMIC AND FINANCIAL ADVICE, TRANSPORT PLANNING AND PUBLIC ENGAGEMENT

A NEW CITY SPANNING 6,845 HECTARES

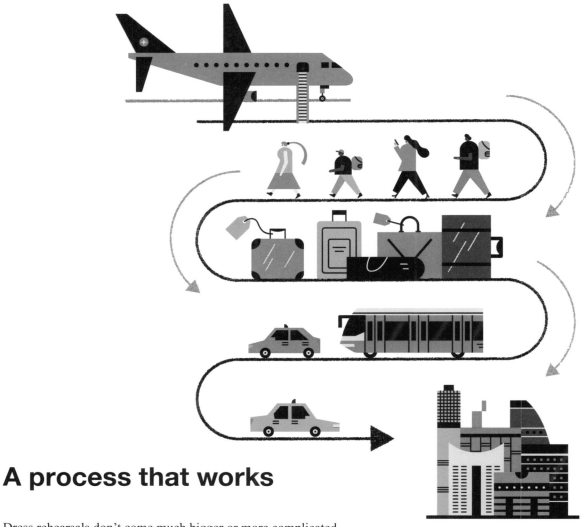

A process that works

Dress rehearsals don't come much bigger or more complicated than the one for the opening of Dubai Airport's new Concourse A. Fifteen million passengers pass through every year, carrying 22m pieces of luggage and boarding 50,000 flights. Clearly, the financial and reputational cost of mistakes is great, so everything has to run smoothly from day one.

Our Operational Readiness, Activation and Transition (ORAT) team started running trials involving the complex integration of systems, processes and staff up to two years before the opening. It wasn't just the main elements, such as the new rail link, baggage systems and boarding gates, that were tested. Our opening-day simulations involved mock passengers and all the typical stresses of a live airport. As a result, problems were highlighted and corrected before the first passenger arrived.

We have done exactly the same at key points during Dubai Airport's £5bn expansion. With more than 50 years of knowledge and experience in airport design and project management, we ensured an unbroken process from development to operation. That's good for passengers and great for the reputation of the airport.

Project name: Operational Readiness, Activation and Transition, Dubai International Airport Concourse A
Designed for: Dubai Airports

Safety by design

Designing for safety has long been part of our heritage. From the creation of car-crash simulation programmes with Jaguar in the 1980s to our work in seismic technologies that help buildings better withstand earthquakes, our focus has been on improving our knowledge to find answers to complex questions.

Calling on our expertise in this area, we are currently developing ways to improve the safety of train carriages.

Using cutting-edge software, we can simulate the effect of crashes or explosions on carriages. This allows us to make informed design choices to improve safety. In particular, our work has focused on simulating the effect of a blast in a carriage. What we learn from this can help inform the design of ever-safer rolling stock. For example, it could be designed to better protect travellers from shrapnel.

Once we've designed and analysed our ideas using the software, we graduate to real train carriage prototypes to prove our ideas work.

The research has implications far beyond transport. It helps us design better products and processes. It's a design for life.

Project name: Passenger Railcar Blast Vulnerability
Designed for: US Transportation Security Administration
Designed with: Transportation Technology Center Inc.

CONCRETE
STRUCTURE

THERMAL
MASS
NIGHT-TIME
COOLING

LOW-
ENERGY
LIGHTING
↓ ↓ ↓ ↓

FRESH
AIR AND
DAYLIGHT
IN →

SIMPLE, PASSIVE
FAÇADE

NATURAL
VENTILATION
WHEN YOU
WANT IT

SOLAR
SHADING
WHERE IT'S
NEEDED

GLAZING
WHERE IT
COUNTS

DURABLE AND
AESTHETICALLY
PLEASING

COOLING
FROM THE SLAB
↓ ↓ ↓

↑
3.5m
HIGH CEILINGS
↓

↑
POWER
AND DATA
CABLES
IN THE
FLOOR

The future works

Can you look to the past to create the commercial buildings of the future? The White Collar Factory concept takes inspiration from its industrial forebears. Drawing on the last century's manufacturing spaces, it creates a new space for the modern worker: a space that offers plenty of room, natural ventilation and lots of daylight.

This blueprint for future commercial building design was developed for Derwent London. The goal was to anticipate tenant needs before they are expressed, rather than simply responding to existing commercial office design trends. To achieve this, we focused on five principles: high ceilings; the thermal mass of the building structure; a simple, passive façade; flexible floorplates; and smart servicing.

To help turn the concept into the reality of a 16-storey office tower in London's Tech City district, Derwent London built a fully functional, temporary prototype that allowed us to test our design. It proved to be a success. With 3.5m-high ceilings and high windows, the thermal mass of the concrete construction keeps temperatures consistent. Water runs through pipes in the concrete slabs, providing cooling. Openable windows allow the building's users to opt for natural ventilation when outside conditions are suitable. Mechanical ventilation will serve office areas further from the windows and the whole office when windows are closed.

For the prototype, we created a smart servicing app that allows people to see how the space is operating and adjust controls for improved comfort and energy performance.

At White Collar Factory, smart technology mixes with old-school rules about quality spaces and passive design. Together, they create the workplace of the future.

Project name: White Collar Factory
Designed for: Derwent London
Designed with: Allford Hall Monaghan Morris

Clover Moore

Designing tomorrow's city

In a wonderful image used by Dr Liu Thai Ker, chairman of Singapore's Centre for Liveable Cities, the city is portrayed as humankind's largest piece of industrial design. Like any good piece of design, it has criteria to fulfil: to be user-friendly; to function well; and to look good.

Cities are cultural, artistic and intellectual centres with galleries, museums, educational institutions and newspapers in addition to their sheer density of people and ideas. Cities are also the economic engine of most states and countries. The City of Sydney is an economic powerhouse that generates AUS$100bn worth of economic activity. This represents 8% of Australia's GDP.

After being elected Lord Mayor, one of my first actions was to create our City of Villages to recognise and protect the unique character and identity of each part of the new City of Sydney. We've upgraded main streets, restored historic town halls, and created pocket parks and playgrounds across our villages and central business district.

A successful city needs a plan for the future. Ours is Sustainable Sydney 2030, which was developed after the largest ever community consultation in the city's history. It continues to guide our work today.

Sustainable Sydney 2030 is the cornerstone of everything we do. It is focused on the long-term issues that help make our city a desirable place to live and work. This includes active transport options, a rich cultural life, a sustainable environment, excellent community facilities and high-quality design in both the public and private sector.

Such long-term planning is important to the liveability of any city. A long-term view examines how a city will grow in a sustainable, 'liveable' way. Sydney in 2030 will be the culmination of our work today to build a green, global and connected city. It will be a city in which there is greater urban density, with 80% of the city's residents living in apartments by 2030, up from 70% today. This will include 54,000 residents of the AUS$8bn Green Square project, to which we are contributing AUS$440m.

While facilitating this urbanisation, we are mindful of the need to keep housing affordable, otherwise we risk losing average wage earners and becoming an enclave just for the very wealthy. Our plan includes a clear commitment to deliver affordable housing.

In our city's future, an increasing number of journeys by residents and workers will be made by bike, on foot and on light rail, particularly the new system between Kingsford and Circular Quay, to which we are contributing AUS$220m, and which is scheduled for completion in 2019.

The Sydney of the future will be one that builds on our status as the leading location for the digital economy in Australia. And it will build on the growth of the creative industries we have fostered in the last ten years, with the city set to invest a further AUS$500m on additional cultural and community initiatives over the next ten years.

By 2030, the number of new jobs in our city will have grown by 100,000.

Perhaps most importantly, our city of the future will be one that plays its part in international efforts to avoid dangerous climate change. By 2030, we will have reduced greenhouse gas emissions across the City of Sydney Local Government by 70% from 2006 levels.

Climate change is the greatest challenge for Sydney, as it is for cities around the world.

Cities take up around 2% of the space we have, but contribute about 80% of the pollution that is driving climate change. It is in our cities that we have the greatest opportunities to take action, and we are committed to doing so. We've already reduced emissions by 20% since 2006 and projects are under way to achieve 29% reduction in the coming years. The city is an active member of the C40 Cities Climate Leadership Group, established in 2005 to reduce greenhouse gas emissions and address climate risks and impacts.

All these things are important. But it is diversity that lies at the heart of what makes cities such fantastic, rewarding places to live. The mosaic of nearly 200 different nationalities that live in a global city like Sydney helps make it a social and cultural smorgasbord of people, ideas and events. Diversity of choice – be it culinary, cultural, sporting or artistic – is also a key feature of great cities. And great cities thrive on diversity of opportunity through the jobs and economic activity that they create.

Clover Moore is an Australian politician. She has been Lord Mayor of the City of Sydney since 2004. She leads the implementation of Sustainable Sydney 2030.

Making work safer

Tragedy can often bring out the best in people. After the 2013 Rana Plaza factory collapse in Bangladesh, we put out a call for help to all disciplines across the firm. Soon, we'd assembled a team of experts eager to help devise and deliver a swift, practical and accurate way of assessing the structural safety of the country's clothing factories.

Switching our focus from ongoing fire safety audits of factories for Inditex, a global fashion retailer, our engineers worked at speed to survey and assess 120 buildings in a short timeframe. After developing an assessment methodology, supported by data from the Bangladesh University of Engineering and Technology, we visited factories to carry out structural surveys. We categorised factories according to risk of failure, using load assessments, design and construction documentation and observations of structural behaviour.

The industry became a safer place because action was taken; some structures needed strengthening, others were condemned.

>

The Rana Plaza building
in Dhaka collapsed on
24 April 2013, killing
1,129 garment workers

About 4m people, mostly women, are employed in Bangladesh's clothing and textile industry

Our work grew to cover factories of the Accord, an umbrella group of 200 fashion brand suppliers in Bangladesh, which also adopted our methodology. Next, we collaborated with the International Labour Organization and the Bangladeshi government safety initiative, surveying buildings not covered by the private sector. To date, we have been involved in the assessment of 1,000 buildings.

For us, success meant combining short-term preventative action with the long-term sustainability of the buildings and the wider industry. Where before there was no standardised way of assessing factory buildings, Bangladesh's clothing industry now has a practical, efficient methodology and is a safer place to work.

Project name: Inditex Fire Emergency Plans; Inditex Structural Surveys; Accord Review of Standards; Accord Structural Surveys; ILO Quality Assurance for Safety Inspections
Designed for: Inditex; Stichting Bangladesh Accord Foundation; UN International Labour Organization

Bangladesh's ready-made garment industry accounts for
78%
of total exports...

...and is the country's biggest export earner:
US$21.51bn
(2012/13)

Almost
200
international brands signed the Accord on Fire and Building Safety in Bangladesh...

...in more than
20
countries in Europe, North America, Asia and Australia

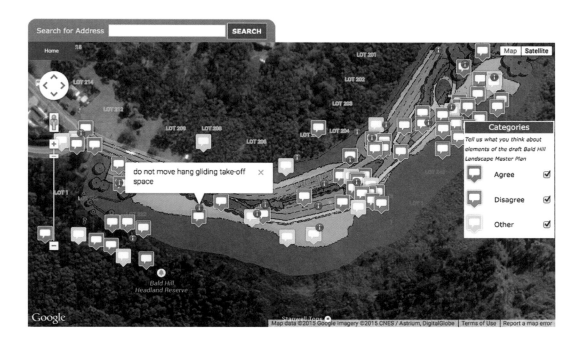

Talking gets results

Communication is key to any successful project. At Bald Hill Reserve, south of Sydney, we were asked to develop a new landscape masterplan. Its aim was to protect the beauty of the site and manage visitors.

We knew people would have something to say about this well-loved site, so we helped them get involved in the design process by using CollabMap, our online map-based community engagement tool. This allows locals to easily contribute their ideas and feedback without having to go to workshops or traditional town hall meetings.

And it works for us too, giving us access to a greater range of opinions, aspirations and concerns. Harnessing this communication, we can make thoughtful, relevant design decisions and then refine them using people's feedback.

Project name: Bald Hill Landscape Masterplan
Designed for: Wollongong City Council, Australia

Managing vibrations

California might be the home of the Beach Boys' hit 'Good Vibrations', but people who live and work in cities know that vibrations aren't always good. In fact, they made the job of constructing a multimodal transit centre, surrounded by high-rises in a built-up area of San Francisco, even more challenging.

Both a commuter line and the high-speed rail link between San Francisco and Los Angeles will terminate in the basement of the new Transbay Transit Center. But when we started work, the site was made up of 60m of old foundations and reclaimed land, sand, Bay mud, clay and lumps of the underlying bedrock that had been transported by glacial meltwater.

It was a precision job that involved excavations to 20m deep and 55m wide, cutting across three city streets. To make this process possible, we developed Global Analyzer. This network of wireless sensors detected ground movements and water pressure across the site and collated this real-time data, alerting engineers to any problems early on.

Alongside this work, our soil structure analysis provided a detailed understanding of how vibrations might affect the new centre and the surrounding structures. It's enabled us to design protection for the site and existing buildings.

Both approaches will benefit San Francisco and its expanded transit system. They will also ripple through other cities wrestling with the challenges posed by poor soil, dense buildings and bad vibrations.

Project name: Transbay Transit Center
Designed for: The Transbay Joint Powers Authority
Designed with: Pelli Clarke Pelli Architects

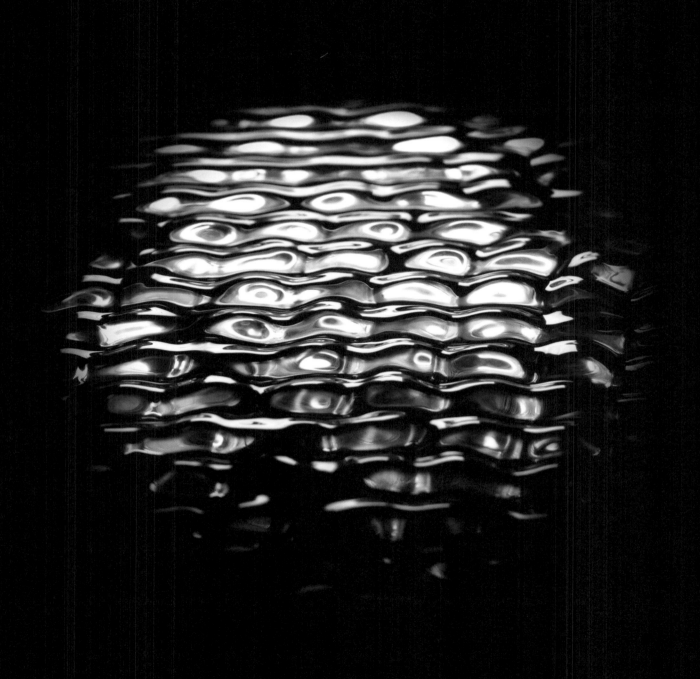

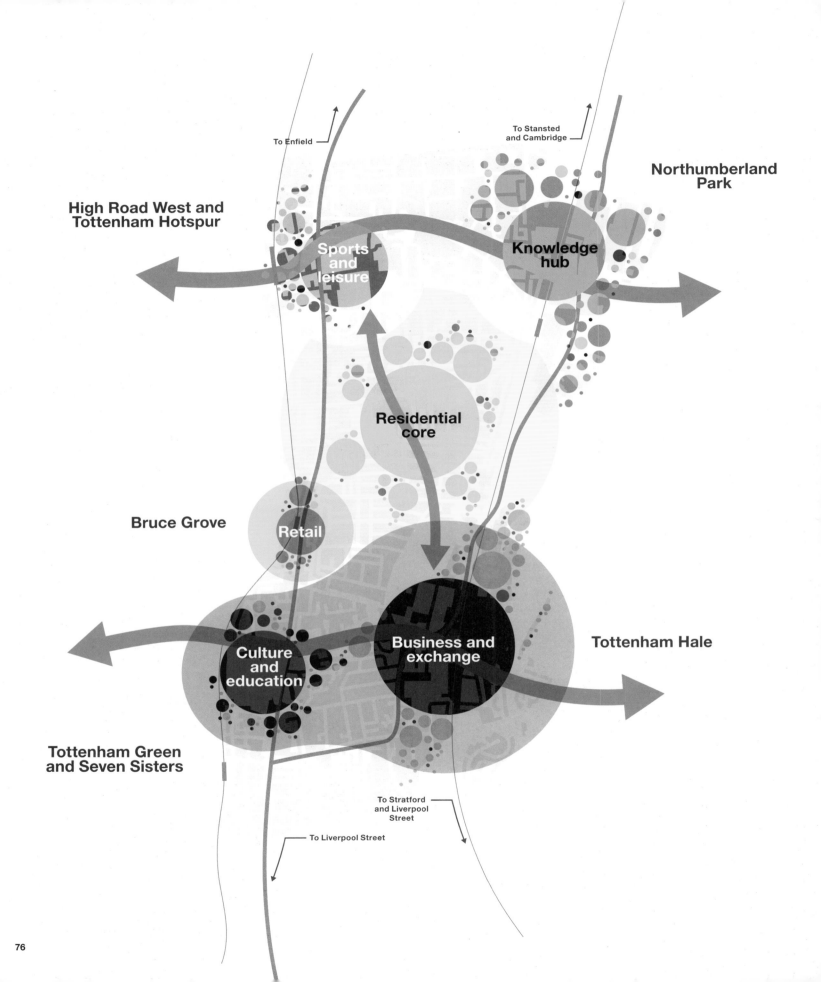

To Enfield

To Stansted
and Cambridge

**Northumberland
Park**

**High Road West and
Tottenham Hotspur**

Sports
and
leisure

**Knowledge
hub**

**Residential
core**

Bruce Grove

Retail

Business and
exchange

Tottenham Hale

Culture
and
education

**Tottenham Green
and Seven Sisters**

To Stratford
and Liverpool
Street

To Liverpool Street

A spur for change

The 2011 riots brought north London's Tottenham into national headlines. One positive result of this was investment from the Mayor of London and Haringey Council to rebuild damaged properties and for the long-term regeneration of the area.

To remove some of the historic economic risk for investors in this area, we helped secure a £500m government loan guarantee for key infrastructure. We then began drawing up a strategy for regeneration.

We worked with a diverse local consortium. This included Homes for Haringey, which works with young adults, including ex-offenders who were involved in the riots; and the Dandelion Project, an online magazine run by schoolchildren. The aim was to engage the local community in plans for the area and knit together small and large projects to create a coordinated approach. It worked.

The masterplan for High Road West shows how we could use the proposed £430m Tottenham Hotspur football stadium as a catalyst for better housing, more job opportunities and a safer, greener community.

We also carried out a study of the high street. This looked at ways to mix work spaces, such as recording studios and furniture workshops, with leisure and retail uses, boosting their visibility and bringing back a sense of pride to the local neighbourhoods.

This work, along with masterplans, transport, business and housing studies, is contributing to Haringey Council's long-term plans for change in north Tottenham. Between now and 2025, 5,000 jobs will be created, 10,000 homes will be built and more green public space will become part of the landscape, making it a better place to live and work.

Project name: Tottenham Regeneration Strategy
Designed for: Greater London Authority; London Borough of Haringey
Designed with: S333; Jones Lang LaSalle; Landolt+Brown; Architecture 00; Space Syntax; Useful Simple

"Ever since the regeneration, there have been a lot of things going on for the community. It is a lot more peaceful. I feel there is less crime and you feel safer. You can go about your day and feel normal."

Fiona Namale, student

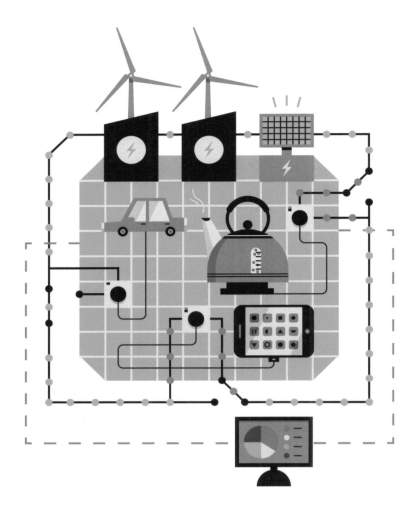

Energy in the right place

Cities are getting smarter. In China, residents will soon be able
to find out exactly how they use energy in their home at any given
time. In fact, they will be able to monitor their habits over any day,
week or year.

Hansung City in Qingdao has asked us to make it a test site for
micro-energy grid (MEG) technology in a bid to drive down carbon
emissions and reduce costs. Energy will be directed where and when
it is needed. Carbon savings of up to 25% are forecast through the
behavioural change that will come from simply knowing where
every kilowatt hour of energy is being used at any one time.

We created the masterplan – in collaboration with a group of
Korean businesses, led by Samsung – to demonstrate that it
is possible to run a city of 100,000 people on a micro-grid. This
smart, energy-efficient technology could change the behaviour of
city residents for the better.

Project name: KMEG, Hansung City
Designed for: Qingdao Local Government
Designed with: Samsung

Resilient

www.arup.com/designbook

Judith Rodin
Building resilient cities

From funding Jane Jacobs in the 1960s to write *The Death and Life of Great American Cities* to the launch of our 100 Resilient Cities Challenge in 2013, The Rockefeller Foundation has long viewed cities as networks of interdependent systems, laboratories of innovation and centres of opportunity and prosperity.

And for the first time in history, half the planet now lives in cities, a number expected to grow to more than 70% by 2050. This rapidly accelerating urbanisation – along with globalisation and climate change – places greater pressures on urban systems, further exacerbated by rising sea levels, air pollution and flooding.

According to data compiled by Swiss Re from more than 600 of the world's largest metropolitan areas, nearly 400m urban dwellers are in peril from coastal and river flooding. And it's not just natural disasters – not a week goes by without disruption to a city somewhere in the world, whether it's civil unrest, a cyber attack or a failure of infrastructure. In addition to one-off catastrophic events, there are also the slower-burning stresses that weaken a city over time – poverty, violence and traffic congestion.

In other words, crisis is becoming the new normal. At The Rockefeller Foundation, we recognise that in order to address the social and economic challenges facing humanity, cities need to build greater resilience against a range of vulnerabilities, and in the process, unleash new opportunities.

One area in need of such solutions is water. This year the World Economic Forum cited water crises as the number one global risk in terms of potential impact – more serious than energy or international conflict.

Changing climate is shifting rainfall patterns dramatically, meaning more drought in some places and more rain in others. And the risk of social unrest and even civil conflicts is greater where competition for water is fiercest. What's more, cities greatly underestimate their water risks. Among the 800 cities that applied to our 100 Resilient Cities Network, 60% counted coastal or river flooding among the four most significant potential crises. In fact, 85% were at risk.

Cities must learn to live with water, not simply 'pave, pipe and pump' to keep it out. Many are finding innovative ways of doing just that, from integrating stormwater infrastructure with other types of infrastructure, such as car parks or green spaces, to integrating hard and soft solutions, such as oyster reefs, to protect key assets.

Across all of these solutions, cities are reaping a resilience dividend – the benefits that come from investing in resilience in the good times, not just the bad times. This includes job creation, ecosystem strengthening, and new opportunities for economic inclusion.

Addressing water crises is only one way in which cities can generate resilience dividends. For example, in Medellín, Colombia, the government's investment in transit infrastructure not only connected poor communities on the hillside with economic activity in the valley below – it also brought crime rates down by 90%.

Everyone – business, government, civic society, academia and NGOs – has a role to play in building resilience, and everyone stands to benefit. Because of globalisation, vulnerability in one city can ripple through others. The 2011 floods in Bangkok, Thailand, for example, shut down much of the global supply chain. At the same time, cities can learn from one another, regardless of whether they face the same risks.

Through our 100 Resilient Cities Network and our Asian Cities Climate Change Resilience Network, we're finding that resilience is a great convener, bringing together cities from across regions and ideologies to create solutions to shared challenges. Design competitions, such as Rebuild by Design in the regions in the US affected by Superstorm Sandy, have pioneered new models for partnerships between engineers, architects and local communities. Increasingly, governments around the world are looking to the design community for their expertise.

We have a clear opportunity in front of us – 70% of the infrastructure that will exist in 2050 hasn't been built yet. Together, we can build our cities to grow, transform and thrive in a future very different from our past.

Dr Judith Rodin has been president of The Rockefeller Foundation since 2005. She is a former president of the University of Pennsylvania and dean of the graduate school at Yale University. She serves on the boards of a number of public companies and non-profit institutions.

The C40 cities have united
to combat climate change

Shining example

Few organisations are as ambitious as the C40 Cities Climate Leadership Group, a global network of cities committed to working together to reduce greenhouse gas emissions and climate risks. Our role is to collate data from these cities, analyse what the figures mean and create a report that other cities can use for planning.

In this case, we took data from more than 200 cities and created models looking ahead to 2050. We then extrapolated this data to make estimates for a further 3,000 cities.

If those 3,000 cities were making the same efforts as the C40 network, we would make significant steps towards avoiding catastrophic climate change.

The report, *Global Aggregation of City Climate Commitments*, underlined the importance of cities in the war against climate change. By working together, we can help cities to win this battle.

Project name: Working Together: Global Aggregation of City Climate Commitments
Designed for: C40 Cities Climate Leadership Group
Designed with: Michael R Bloomberg, UN Secretary-General's Special Envoy for Cities and Climate Change; UN Habitat; UCLG; WRI; ICLEI; CDP; carbonn

What makes a city resilient?

What makes some cities better able to weather the shocks and stresses of natural disasters, climate change, food and water shortages and energy security?

Working with The Rockefeller Foundation, we set out to answer these questions. Our aim was to create a City Resilience Index to enable cities to understand and measure their resilience. Armed with that knowledge, cities are better placed to make investment decisions that ensure they survive and thrive whatever happens.

The launch of the City Resilience Framework brought together research and fieldwork in six cities: Concepción in Chile, Cali in Colombia, New Orleans in the US, Cape Town in South Africa, Surat in India and Semarang in Indonesia. Our work revealed that resilience not only depends on protective infrastructure and emergency planning, but also on social stability and empowered stakeholders. Integrated planning and robust communication networks are essential. Resilience also depends on specific qualities such as redundancy, resourcefulness and inclusivity.

The City Resilience Framework captures the critical issues that contribute to a city's 'immune system'. It is already being adopted by cities and city-makers, enabling them to make better-informed decisions that will help secure their future. It will form the basis of the City Resilience Index.

Project name: City Resilience Index
Designed for: The Rockefeller Foundation
Designed with: The Rockefeller Foundation

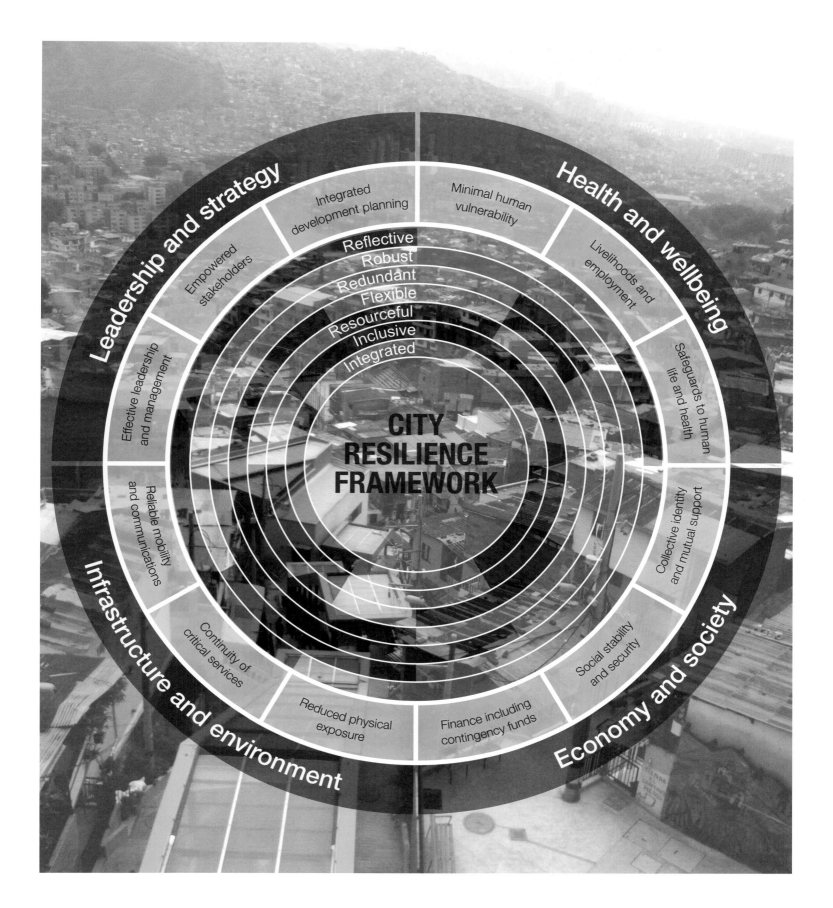

Leadership and strategy

Health and wellbeing

Infrastructure and environment

Economy and society

CITY
RESILIENCE
FRAMEWORK

Integrated development planning

Minimal human vulnerability

Empowered stakeholders

Livelihoods and employment

Effective leadership and management

Safeguards to human life and health

Reliable mobility and communications

Collective identity and mutual support

Continuity of critical services

Social stability and security

Reduced physical exposure

Finance including contingency funds

Reflective
Robust
Redundant
Flexible
Resourceful
Inclusive
Integrated

Climate challenges

Some cities face specific resilience challenges. For ten cities in India, Indonesia, Thailand and Vietnam, the greatest threat is climate change.

Our work with The Rockefeller Foundation has led to the creation of the Asian Cities Climate Change Resilience Network. It enables communities and cities to better manage the disruption caused by their changing climate.

The aim is to build resilience by helping local partner organisations better understand and tackle the risks and uncertainties of future climate change. For example, in Gorakhpur, India, we are working with the Gorakhpur Environmental Action Group to identify ways to respond to the health risks of seasonal waterlogging.

We are also preparing for the expected increase in rainfall by improving waste management, clearing drains and reducing rubbish. Meanwhile, in Semarang,

Indonesia, we have joined forces with vulnerable community groups to improve their flood resilience. This involves providing training and information on how best to prepare for and respond to emergencies.

By promoting knowledge-sharing and encouraging joint working to solve problems, we have helped communities understand the power of collaboration. The lessons learned will help these cities – and many more – be better prepared to respond to the challenges and stresses of climate change.

Project name: Asian Cities Climate Change Resilience Network (ACCCRN)
Designed for: The Rockefeller Foundation
Designed with: Gorakhpur Environmental Action Group; TARU Leading Edge Pvt Ltd; MercyCorps Indonesia; Thailand Environment Institute; ISET-International Vietnam; ICLEI – Local Governments for Sustainability; International Institute for Environment and Development

Community matters

Resilience involves people, not just infrastructure. Our work with the International Federation of the Red Cross and Red Crescent Societies is proof positive of this. Together, we are supporting community-based disaster risk reduction programmes in Asia and Latin America.

In the wake of the devastating 2004 Indian Ocean tsunami, we were asked to help identify and document the lessons learned. After undertaking this research in Asia, we were able to replicate it in Latin America and the Caribbean to broaden our findings.

Our aim was to define the characteristics of a resilient community as a model to help the development of disadvantaged communities. Factors included social cohesion and infrastructure. Both of these aid a faster bounce-back after incidents.

One community we worked with was in Saint Lucia. Because it has a high degree of social contact, there is a shared sense of responsibility for things like water infrastructure. People are more likely to maintain shared assets such as water sources in their villages, which means they're less liable to fail – and illness is less likely.

Contrast this with some informal settlements in Bogotá, Colombia. Local roads are in disrepair and damaged further by frequent rain. The community didn't know how to mend them and didn't know who to talk to. The Red Cross is ensuring that isolated communities like these have interconnected sources of information that can help them. This provides greater resilience – through infrastructure and people.

Project name: Community-based Disaster Risk Reduction Study
Designed for: International Federation of the Red Cross and Red Crescent Societies
Designed with: Colombian Red Cross Society; Saint Lucia Red Cross; Guatemalan Red Cross

Weathering the storm

In 2012, Hurricane Sandy reminded us that natural disasters can affect even the most developed economies. New York and New Jersey were severely damaged. Our work has focused on small, sustainable interventions that increase both liveability and resilience. Here are three very different projects in New York that show how small initiatives can cleverly – and cumulatively – make a big difference.

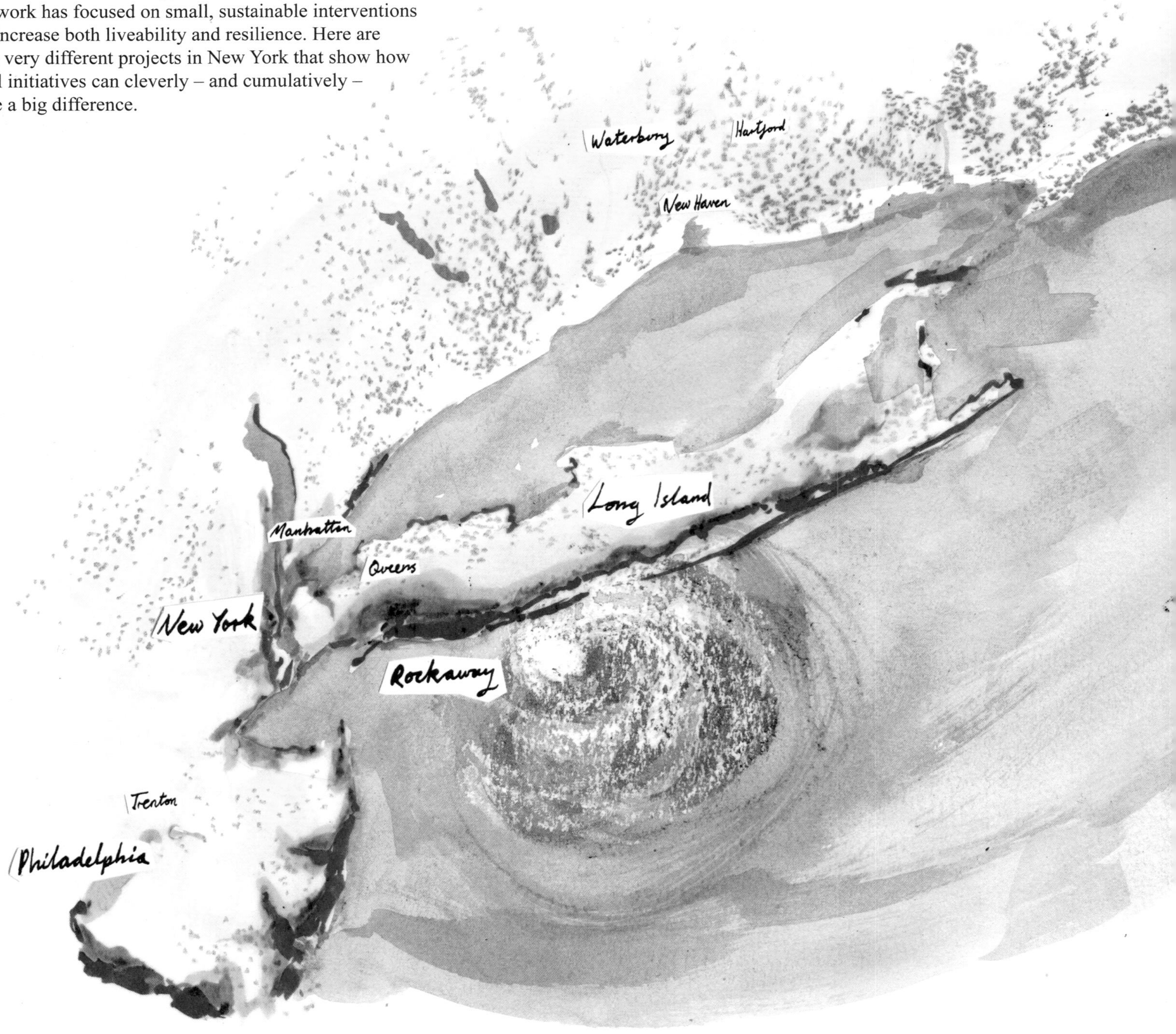

Waterbury

Hartford

New Haven

Long Island

Manhattan

Queens

New York

Rockaway

Trenton

Philadelphia

Working with the tide

The Rockaway peninsula was one of the areas worst affected by Hurricane Sandy. Developers of a flood-prone site on the waterfront held a competition for sustainable and resilient planning and design ideas.

We entered the FAR ROC (For a Resilient Rockaway) competition with Stockholm-based White Arkitekter, proposing ideas that reduce the risk of flooding and allow a quick recovery.

Our proposal was to work with the water rather than try to stop the rising tides and large waves. For those waves that do reach the peninsula, we've designed boardwalks that can ride the storm. These are hinged, allowing them to lift up as water reaches them before falling again.

Our proposals show that innovative ideas can be both sustainable and affordable. Every element of this mixed-use, mixed-income development is designed to create a community that embraces the tides.

>

Project name: FAR ROC (For a Resilient Rockaway)
Designed for: Arverne East LLC
Designed with: White Arkitekter

Potential storm-surge
flooding from hurricanes

Low ⟶ High

Retrofitting resilience

In the days and weeks after Hurricane Sandy, confusion reigned. Residents, property owners and officials were eager to rebuild the city's damaged and vulnerable housing stock. However, no one was exactly sure how the storm had affected residential properties, much less how best to rebuild them stronger and safer. New York's Office of Housing Recovery Operations hired Arup to help find out.

Our team started by pulling together existing data from different city agencies and visiting affected sites across the city. We used the information gleaned from this process to divide the housing stock into 15 different types, from towers to bungalows. We then brought together officials, federal agencies and local designers to develop retrofit strategies that would be viable for each housing type from both a regulatory and an architectural standpoint. Finally, we developed cost estimates for these efforts to help inform New York City's financial requests to the federal government.

In less than four months, we developed an easy-to-read guide that gave city agencies the information they needed to move ahead with housing recovery efforts. The document has since formed the basis of the Department of City Planning's definitive guide for homeowners, developers and government agencies on how to retrofit New York homes.

Project name: Support to the Office of Housing Recovery Operations
Designed for: New York City Office of Housing Recovery Operations; US Federal Emergency Management Agency
Designed with: Architecture Research Office; ATCS; AECOM

On the waterfront

As weather becomes more extreme and sea levels rise, traditional approaches to coastal defences, such as sea walls, are being tested to their limits. That's where the NY Rising Community Reconstruction Program steps in. It's a grassroots planning and implementation initiative created by New York Governor Andrew M Cuomo to rebuild communities affected by recent hurricanes and increase their resilience to future events.

Our role included planning, engineering, consulting and public outreach across five areas – each guided by a committee of local leaders – in Nassau County on Long Island. We facilitated a series of meetings to discuss the real risks that come from living on the waterfront. We organised four public engagement events, allowing hundreds of members of the public to provide input on

resiliency projects. With this knowledge, the committees were able to conceive solutions to improve physical, social and economic resilience. Projects they've requested funding for include solar-powered street lights that work when the power is out, naturalised shorelines and waterways, and programmes to prepare businesses and residents for extreme weather.

Together with the people living in waterfront communities, we've identified short- and long-term ways to improve resilience and increase safety.

Project name: NY Rising Community Reconstruction Program
Designed for: New York State, Governor's Office of Storm Recovery
Designed with: Sasaki Associates

To build high, build low

Torre Reforma is proof that to build high, sometimes you have to build low. To create this world-class skyscraper on Mexico City's shifting ground, we needed a new approach to seismic design.

The effect of an earthquake is like shaking a bowl of jelly: seismic waves deep underground create much more movement on ground level and above.

We therefore turned the site's ten-storey basement to our advantage: the deep structure below ground stabilises the building against this movement. Not only is the skyscraper able to withstand shocks, it also has more leaseable floor space, because less room is taken up with shock absorbers.

Our integrated approach took the best international knowledge and passed it on to local contractors and consultants. It's set a precedent for buildings in the city, showing that world-class thinking can help a growing economy rise even higher.

Project name: Torre Reforma
Designed for: Fondo Hexa SA de CV
Designed with: L Benjamín Romano, LBR&A

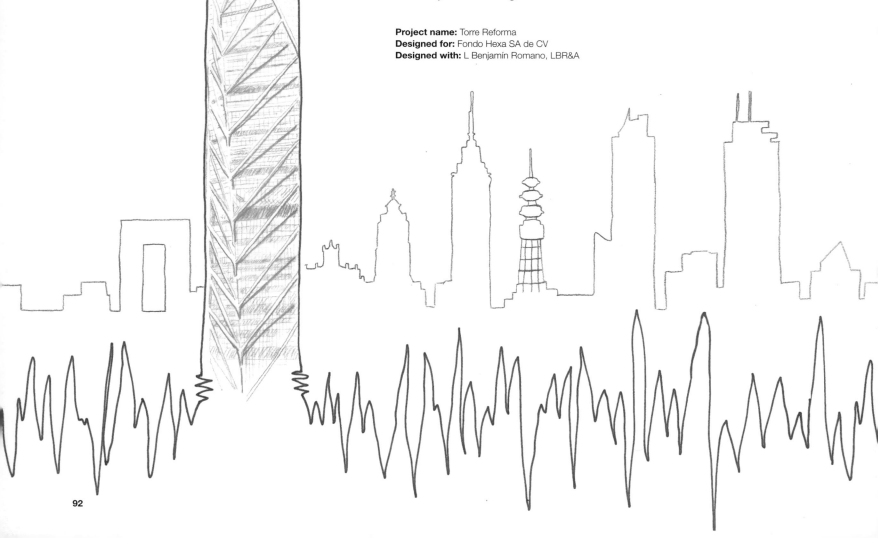

Beautiful

www.arup.com/designbook

A sporting home

Adelaide Oval was once the home ground of the cricketing legend Sir Donald Bradman. So when the Australian city needed to redevelop its sporting facilities, cultural heritage was a consideration. But there was a problem. There was a picturesque, 140-year-old cricket ground in the city centre and an ageing Australian Rules football stadium on the outskirts. It was not feasible to keep both running, yet both were needed.

The answer was to merge the two venues. Instead of designing a new stadium from scratch, we updated the Adelaide Oval cricket ground and made it home to two sports. We engineered two new roofs for the stands. The larger is a 137m cantilever shell construction, supported only along its edge and so reducing the steel needed. The fabric cladding used for the cantilevered roof, which shelters spectators from the rain and shields them from the sun, has further saved on the amount of steel used.

It's a winning solution. The spectator experience has improved and capacity at the world-class stadium has risen from 34,000 to 53,500. The city has not only kept its cultural heritage, it has added to it, because after 40 years of absence, football is returning to the heart of Adelaide. In the process, the city is revitalised through greater footfall to its restaurants, clubs and bars after matches at this iconic arena.

Project name: Adelaide Oval Redevelopment
Designed for: Adelaide Oval Stadium Management Authority; Department of Planning, Transport and Infrastructure (Government of South Australia)
Designed with: Cox Architecture; Walter Brooke; Hames Sharley; Wallbridge & Gilbert

Australian cricketing legend Sir Donald Bradman at the Adelaide Oval, 1934

Thomas Heatherwick
British heritage, global reach

As a London-born designer with a London-based design practice, Thomas Heatherwick has not strayed far from his roots geographically. And yet his designs, which include Al Fayah Park in Abu Dhabi and the UK's Seed Cathedral pavilion at Expo 2010 in Shanghai, not to mention the iconic Olympic Cauldron for London 2012, have ensured a global reputation for Heatherwick Studio.

Heatherwick's influence might be international, but the studio and designer are best known for designs with a UK, and specifically London, identity, such as the Rolling Bridge and the New Bus for London. Heatherwick's work captures the essence of London in striking, world-class designs that also give a strong sense of place. There is a reason for this: "Cities are the most exciting places. It is so important that cities invent their own interesting ways of doing things and don't copy each other," he says.

"So often the aesthetic manifestations of patterns, both public and private, are increasingly similar to other cities around the world. But as humans we are drawn to the odd, the unusual, the idiosyncratic. It is not illogical, barmy or stupid. It is essential food for the imagination of us all."

The Olympic Cauldron is a clear example of a quirky approach that captured worldwide attention. It was experimental. It did not follow the official brief, which stipulated that it should have no moving parts and be located on the roof of the stadium. Yet it was a clear representation of the very best of London design, and achieved its objective of galvanising 204 countries, and bringing them together in the design both metaphorically and literally.

The London 2012 Olympic Games, where the Olympic Cauldron took centre stage, symbolised a turning point for Heatherwick in terms of the importance of designing for his home city. "The Games gave back some confidence and optimism. And the legacy is a major park. One of the most spectacular memories anyone who went to the Games will have is of the wild flowers, which were just stunning."

Heatherwick took that wave of optimism, that sense of London as a city, and is channelling it all into his design for the Garden Bridge, which will span the River Thames. "I grew up in the 1970s and 1980s where the assumption was that Britain – despite being one of the most pioneering, ingenious nations in history – had somehow become a country that you had to leave, and instead go to Paris or Barcelona to see cities that were not letting themselves be stifled by their own history," he says.

The Garden Bridge will be part of London's evolution. "I think this idea has caught many people's imaginations, as it caught mine," he says, adding that in London there is a strong sense of 'north of the river' and 'south of the river', with little to bring these two sides together. "The river has been treated as an obstacle, because it is so wide, so the bridges have been seen as links, not places. And what felt powerful to me was the idea of making a place."

But cities are not only about embracing the new; they should also allow the best of the old to evolve. "The challenge for a city is to dare to have a character," says Heatherwick. "The character is manifested in the people and the spaces for those people. Those two things augment and draw out the idiosyncrasies of the people. They go together."

And that means building on and growing old traditions as well as inventing new ones. "Time goes fast; invent something, keep it going and before you know it, it's a tradition."

The expectation is that the Garden Bridge will encourage people who live in and visit London to embrace the river that runs through its heart. This appreciation will be the litmus test for Heatherwick, whose passion is public projects. "I recognise this is the hardest area," he says. "It is easy to do a project in a gallery, because there is a big bubble telling you the contents are special. But the space around us is the ultimate leveller. I believe a city is an evolving creation, shared by us all. And in some senses there is more celebration of 'city' than ever before. There is more understanding of their magic, and not just of their mundane necessity."

Thomas Heatherwick founded Heatherwick Studio in 1994. He is widely regarded as one of Britain's most gifted and innovative designers.

A new skyline – an old view

The City of London has one of the most famous skylines in the world. Therefore, any change to it must be handled with the utmost care. That's why The Leadenhall Building, a recent addition, was designed to lean politely away from St Paul's Cathedral to avoid obscuring the view of the historic monument from Fleet Street.

Achieving this was a feat of structural engineering. Because of its shape, the building leaned sideways during construction. To counteract this, some of the sloping steel on the side faces was shortened to pull the megaframe back to the vertical. This began when construction of the 48-storey building reached the 19th floor and was repeated every seven storeys.

The building is a nod to the past. Like the neighbouring Lloyd's building and the Centre Pompidou in Paris – both of which we also delivered with Richard Rogers, founder of Rogers Stirk Harbour + Partners – Leadenhall is a skeletal construction, its steel and connections on show. The megaframe connections were modelled and refined using 3D software, so the flow of forces through the connections is as efficient as possible.

Due to the small plot, some 85% of the structure was assembled off-site, an unprecedented amount of prefabrication for a UK high rise. The 224m Leadenhall is proof you can squeeze a new skyscraper into a small space in a crowded city without disrupting the neighbours.

Project name: The Leadenhall Building
Designed for: British Land; Oxford Properties
Designed with: Rogers Stirk Harbour + Partners

Sporting showcase

World-class cities need world-class leisure venues. The government of Singapore wanted to create a new sports facility near the city centre for residents to enjoy. The location made it vital to retain a connection with the city. That's why our horseshoe-shaped design put Singapore's skyline at its centre.

The sports centre is a multifunctional, all-weather hub surrounded by popular restaurants, a skate park, an aquatics centre, a climbing wall, a bowls green, a volleyball court and a library.

The hub is covered with a spectacular moveable roof. Arching over everything, the ultra-thin shell of the roof structure is the world's largest free-standing dome. An engineering feat, its design has reduced the amount of steel needed and is both retractable and open at one end – for that all-important city view.

Spectators in the stadium sit in comfort. The roof provides shade during events and combines with an energy-efficient seat-cooling system to cope with the tropical climate.

The stadium's moveable lower tier means it can host cricket, football and athletics – a world first – as well as entertainment and cultural events.

It's a winning formula. An elegant and versatile sports hub capable of hosting world sporting events. A space for Singaporeans to enjoy.

The iconic structure can be admired from both inside and out.

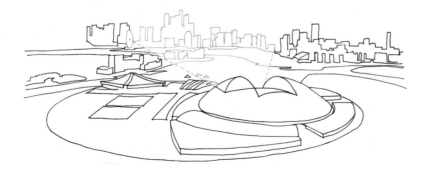

Project name: Singapore Sports Hub
Designed for: Singapore Sports Hub Consortium
Designed with: Dragages Singapore Pte Ltd; Singapore Sports Hub Design Team

Best of both worlds

Charles Rennie Mackintosh's masterly use of light and space is unmistakable. So when a new Glasgow School of Art building (the Reid Building) was commissioned to stand directly opposite the Mackintosh masterpiece, there were two options: do something completely different or take inspiration from it.

The answer was to do both. We worked closely with architect Steven Holl to transform his 'complementary contrast' concept into reality. Starting with his watercolour sketches, the team took inspiration from the famous neighbour, particularly its use of light and space. They then reflected this back in a modern form.

>

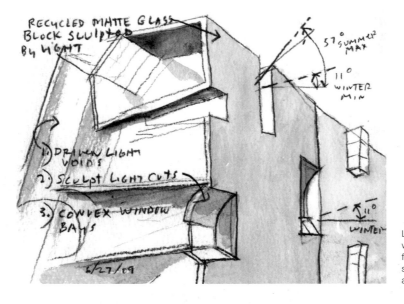

Light and space were top priorities for the new design as shown in this sketch by architect Steven Holl

"The engineering and architecture aren't separated. From the beginning, we had the idea that light would be the structure, and working with Arup we came up with the idea of natural ventilation."

Chris McVoy, Partner in Charge, Steven Holl Architects

"Rennie Mackintosh was pushing the craft of his time. Now it's not so much about craft but about advanced fabrication technology – and we were pushing that. The glass and ghost fittings had never been done before."

Chris McVoy, Partner in Charge, Steven Holl Architects

A key feature of the new Reid Building are the three 'driven voids of light'. These are 5m-diameter monolithic concrete tubes, reminiscent of the Mackintosh library windows. Open to the sky, these perforated tubes are angled at 12 degrees. As well as forming the structure of the building, they capture the low Glaswegian light and provide natural ventilation.

Cutting across, through and around the voids is the 'circuit of connection'. This meandering floating pathway rises up through five storeys, offering views of the studios and leading to a double-height refectory and terrace. This space encourages students to engage with and be inspired by one another's work.

>

"An art school is known for its students, its staff and for what they produce. And also, increasingly – particularly with the Mackintosh building opposite – for the building it inhabits and makes its own."

Seona Reid, Director of GSA 1999–2013

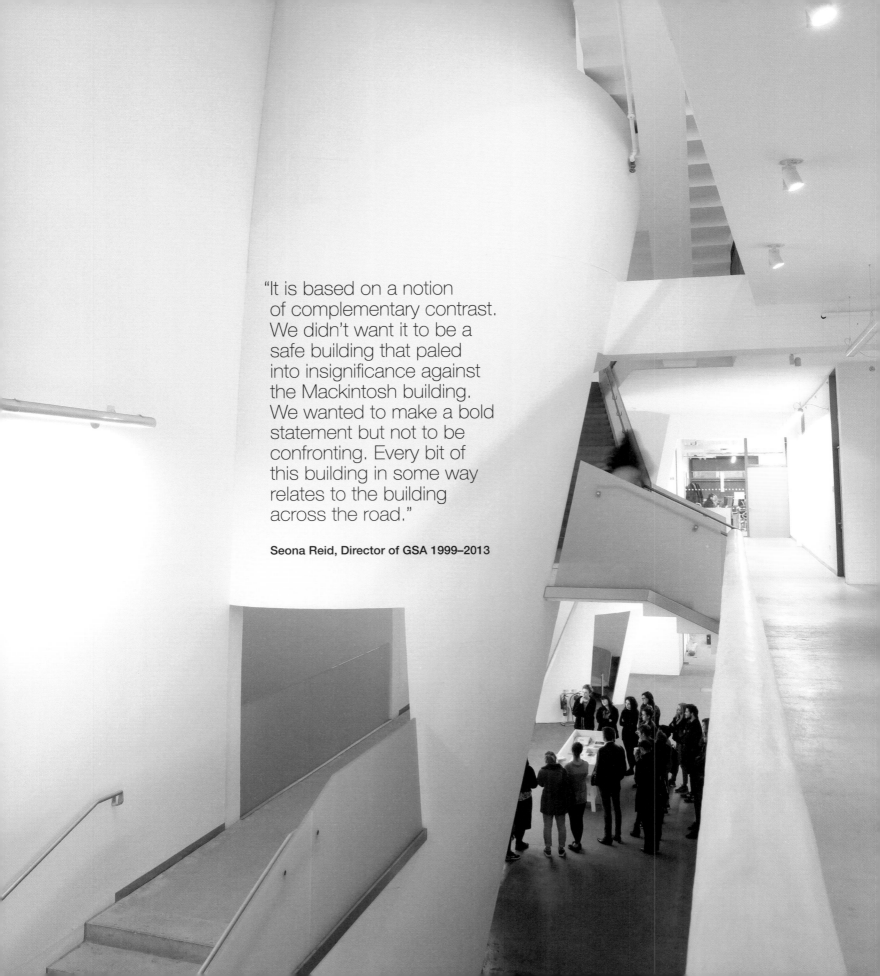

"It is based on a notion
of complementary contrast.
We didn't want it to be a
safe building that paled
into insignificance against
the Mackintosh building.
We wanted to make a bold
statement but not to be
confronting. Every bit of
this building in some way
relates to the building
across the road."

Seona Reid, Director of GSA 1999–2013

"This building has now become the heart of the school. There are so many open places where it's easy to meet people and take a break from work. The way it's laid out means you're always passing people, studios and friendly faces."

Josie Lee, student

The Reid Building is a simple concept that relies on a complex geometric form. Meeting fire safety standards and ventilating the building naturally required some highly technical engineering.

'Contrast' is found in its materials. The Mackintosh has a thick stone skin on a thin steel inner structure. The new building has the opposite: a thin, translucent skin on a thick concrete structure. This plain façade is made up of large sheets of green-grey glass. Behind them are fittings you don't see – 'ghost' fittings. These eliminate the technological feel and position the glass as a silent screen, contrasting with the dark-stoned, heavily detailed Mackintosh.

It's an artistic interpretation of which Charles Rennie Mackintosh, no doubt, would have approved.

Project name: The Reid Building
Designed for: Glasgow School of Art
Designed with: Steven Holl Architects; JM Architects

Evolution for revolution

The entertainment capital of the world is a worthy home for the world's largest observation wheel. Our experience working on the London Eye and the Singapore Flyer helped us to create the Las Vegas High Roller.

Here, London's three-element rim wheel and Singapore's two-element version are further refined into a simple, more elegant design: a single-element tubular rim. This single tube supports 28 spherical cabins that give passengers uninterrupted views of the Las Vegas Strip and beyond.

Designing a wheel of this scale required meticulous attention to detail. The High Roller has been designed and tested to rotate as many as 650,000 times during its lifetime. We specifically designed the wheel to limit changes in stress during each rotation, reducing the potential for the steel to fail through fatigue. To do this, we had to precisely understand and then control all the stresses at every weld, penetration and attachment.

The result is yet another world-class tourist attraction on the Las Vegas Strip, proving evolution and revolution can work together.

Project name: The High Roller
Designed for: Caesars Entertainment
Designed with: The Hettema Group; Klai Juba Wald Architects; Leitner-Poma; Schwager Davis Inc

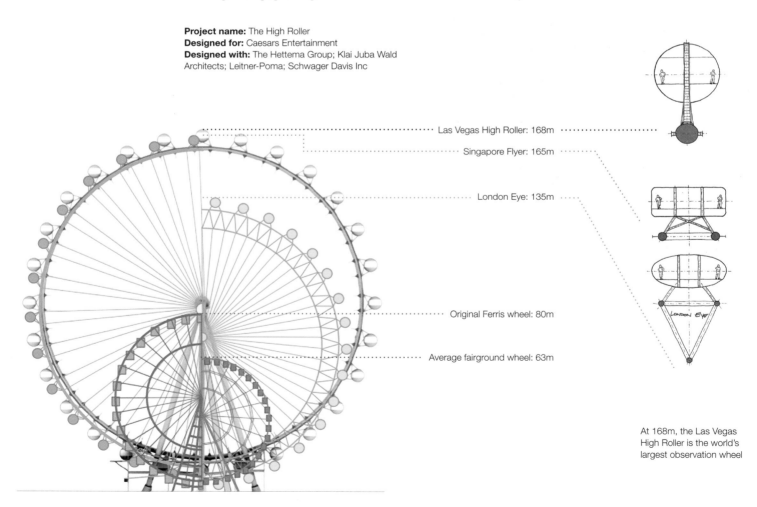

Las Vegas High Roller: 168m

Singapore Flyer: 165m

London Eye: 135m

Original Ferris wheel: 80m

Average fairground wheel: 63m

At 168m, the Las Vegas High Roller is the world's largest observation wheel

An old bridge, a new bridge and a transport problem solved

It's a unique cable-stayed bridge that will also give a new lease of life to the one it is designed to replace. North of Edinburgh, the new Queensferry Crossing was originally planned as a full replacement for the Forth Road Bridge, which is struggling to cope with ongoing maintenance issues and increased traffic levels.

The original brief for the work included a road traffic crossing with the potential to carry a light-rail transit scheme in the future. Working with our partner, Jacobs, we found a way to make it more affordable than the £4bn estimate.

We re-examined previous reports and established that the existing bridge could, with relatively minor changes, carry a light-rail line. It could also be reused to act as a dedicated public transport corridor for buses, pedestrians and cyclists. Retaining limited use of the bridge in this way would reduce the weight of traffic on it and extend its life.

We also showed that overhead signage and mandatory speed controls could regulate the flow of traffic approaching and crossing the Forth, especially at peak times. This would maximise capacity while minimising the new roadworks required.

Our approach allowed us to streamline the design of the new crossing. By reducing the profile of the towers and deck, we cut down the quantities of material needed.

The result will be a stunning piece of new design, a highly effective and efficient new bridge and a repurposed existing landmark. What's more, the project will cost well under half the original estimate. When it opens in 2016, it will be a tale with a very happy ending.

Project name: Forth Replacement Crossing Project
Designed for: Transport Scotland
Designed with: Jacobs Engineering UK Limited

The first performances at the National Taichung Theater took place in 2014

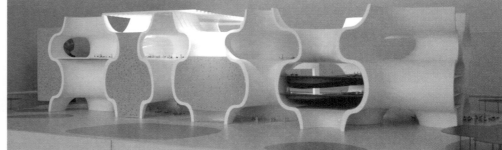

The 'unbuildable' building

They said it couldn't be built. But they were wrong. Toyo Ito's National Taichung Theater, Taiwan, is an extraordinary design: a double-curved concrete shell that forms a continuous shape and serves as the building's structure, as well as its floors and walls.

Our challenge was to bring this bold vision to life. This was no easy feat. Instead of relying solely on 3D models, we combined computer modelling with physical prototypes to develop a new construction technique.

The solution was low-tech. The building's structure is based around a pre-formed steel cage with three layers of mesh on each side. Concrete is poured in and held by the mesh without using complex formwork. It's a simple recipe that results in a complex architectural form.

>

The final venue is six storeys high and topped with a roof garden. It contains three auditoriums, a 2,014-seat grand theatre and an 800-seat playhouse, as well as numerous restaurants and cafés. It represents the dawn of a new cultural age for Taichung. A symbol of success, it is already an unmistakable part of the cityscape. For us, it is a reminder that anything is possible.

Architect Toyo Ito calls his creation 'The Sound Cave'

Project name: National Taichung Theater
Designed for: Taichung City Government, Taiwan
Designed with: Toyo Ito & Associates, Architects

Future

www.arup.com/designbook

Capital gains

Pretoria, the capital of South Africa, reflects the enormous change within the country – both historically and today. In Tshwane, the central area of the city, there was a need for affordable urban redevelopment to address the challenges created by rapid change.

In recent years, this area has seen an exodus of people and businesses, with businesses and government departments relocating outside the city centre. As a result, the quality of the urban environment has suffered, and crime levels have increased. Despite this, a number of areas of the city show stronger social and economic activity than others. Our plan for Tshwane centred on these areas as they will deliver change most effectively, creating the market conditions for wider transformation. It should give businesses and government the confidence needed to reinvest in the centre.

Mixed-use developments, infrastructure and urban management are at the heart of the plan. Many of the main streets have been given new public areas, and a new transit network is being put in place.

Green spaces and areas for recreation are improved with a green infrastructure network running through the city. At a local level, many of the long urban city blocks are being opened up into shorter blocks – boosting both connectivity and safety. Small spaces and urban plazas are the centre of cultural activity and public art.

The result is a plan that prioritises people and sustainability. It maintains the culture and ethos of this historic city, all while turning it into a place people want to live and work in and visit. Pretoria is changing again: into a real 21st-century African capital city.

Project name: Tshwane Inner City Regeneration Project
Designed for: City of Tshwane

Keeping pace with change

The renaissance of Bilbao began in the 1990s. It received a boost the following decade, when work began to develop better infrastructure and attract younger workers, yet maintain the city's identity.

We worked on a masterplan for Basauri, an old industrial area. This 65ha urban regeneration project aimed to improve connectivity, mainly through rail.

We devised several financially sustainable, self-sufficient phases for development. Each of these was designed to work alone if financing for other phases didn't happen. So when the 2008 financial crisis hit, the project was only slowed, rather than halted. The plans will have lasting benefits for residents and the city because of this measured, steady approach.

Using knowledge and experience from our work in cities across the globe, we injected the latest thinking in environment, climate change and resilience. This thinking has also been applied to other projects we've worked on in Bilbao.

For example, at Zorrozaurre, we are providing engineering support to Zaha Hadid's masterplan for the peninsula. Then there's Olebeaga, where we are helping reinvigorate a steeply sloped area dominated by large infrastructure. And finally, there's Philippe Starck's conversion of Alhóndiga Bilbao, an old warehouse, into a cultural and leisure centre.

As anyone who has visited Bilbao will tell you, it's a city well on its way to complete transformation.

Project name: Integrated Study for the Regeneration of Basauri
Designed for: Bilbao Ría 2000

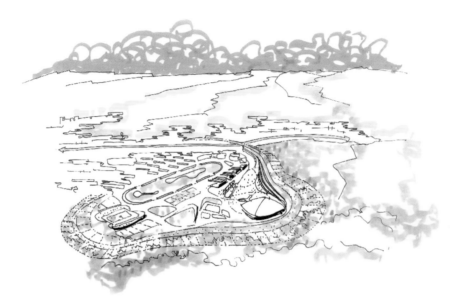

A major regeneration
initiative in the making,
as shown in this sketch
by Rogers Stirk Harbour
+ Partners

Blueprint for regeneration

Briefs that evolve sometimes make for the most interesting – and ambitious – projects. This was certainly true of La Rinconada in Caracas. What started as the construction of a new bus interchange quickly transformed into a major regeneration initiative.

The project now includes housing, parks, a 50,000-seat football stadium and even the retrofitting of architectural masterpieces. It has a focus on social inclusion and returning space to the diverse local community.

For this project, we partnered with the architecture firm Rogers Stirk Harbour + Partners and other stakeholders, including national government and barrio community managers.

The plans have the need to drive change at their heart. They were heavily influenced by environment, transport, knowledge, community and recreation. Our inclusive approach meant the plan could be bold.

We identified smaller quick wins that would immediately improve quality of life, such as pop-up gardens, community parks and the retrofit of existing government buildings.

The resulting masterplan will transform La Rinconada. In fact, it is already becoming a socially inclusive area, brimming with facilities and opportunities for residents.

Project name: La Rinconada Masterplan
Designed for: Municipio Bolivariano Libertador del Distrito Capital, Caracas, Venezuela
Designed with: Rogers Stirk Harbour + Partners; Arquitectura Agronomia

Preparing for population growth

It's a challenge familiar to many cities: as populations rise, can existing infrastructure cope? Melbourne's population is growing faster than that of any other Australian city. If trends continue, by 2051 it will be the country's most populous, the number of its residents almost doubling to 8m people. A regional group of planners in Northern Melbourne realised they needed a robust approach to understanding current and future infrastructure investments.

Using workshops, research, demographic and transport modelling and stakeholder interviews, we compiled a 50-year plan with priorities in the short, medium and long term. The first wave of the plan focuses on transport and social infrastructure projects, such as improving the tram operations and boosting age care facilities. The second wave involves enhancing the rail network, including a rail link to the airport. The final wave – over 20 to 50 years – involves a road upgrade, a new interstate freight terminal and a rail network upgrade.

A long-term infrastructure plan enables city leaders to invest in developing infrastructure at the right time. For Melbourne, it will mean remaining one of the world's most liveable cities.

Project name: NORTHERN HORIZONS – 50 Year Infrastructure Strategy for Melbourne's North
Designed for: NORTH Link; Northern Melbourne RDA Committee; La Trobe University; the eight Northern Melbourne municipalities of Banyule, Darebin, Hume, Mitchell, Moreland, Nillumbik, Yarra and Whittlesea
Designed with: MGS Architects

The population of Melbourne's North will increase from approximately 1m residents to approximately 1.6m by 2051

By 2051, the population in the region aged 60 or over will increase from approximately 157,000, or 17% of the population, to just under 400,000, or 25% of the population

Melbourne's North will require an additional 61 nurseries, 55 kindergartens and 21 primary schools by 2021

By 2021 Melbourne's North will require an additional 56 new community centres across the region

A train that gives heart

What a difference a train makes. The arrival of the HS2 high-speed train line will create a once-in-a lifetime opportunity for Solihull. But careful planning will be required to capitalise on the economic opportunities.

Connectivity and land availability mean that Solihull is already an attractive place for business. Situated in the middle of the UK, it is home to Birmingham Airport, its adjacent station, the National Exhibition Centre and the M6 and M42 corridors. But when it becomes the first stop outside London on HS2, it will be even more appealing.

We've helped to prepare an economic strategy that will leverage potential growth without sacrificing Solihull's rural and urban character. A masterplan for a hub around the new station identifies the infrastructure needed to capitalise on HS2 and Solihull's existing assets. It includes plans to integrate the proposed station into the town's current transport network and link it to the airport. Retail expansion is also planned. Our proposals are the result of ongoing consultation and workshops with the local community.

The economic strategy has secured political support for the plans. It is a model of fully integrated urban planning, pre-empting the arrival of HS2 and all the benefits that will come with it. So stand back – there's a train approaching.

Project name: UK Central (previously, M42 Economic Gateway)
Designed for: Solihull Metropolitan Borough Council
Designed with: Jones Lang LaSalle; Ecorys; PwC

Small design,
big impact

In the ancient shopping street of Dashilar in Beijing, a low-tech piece of street furniture has put a smile on the face of pedestrians, cyclists and drivers alike. As part of the Dashilar Pilot preservation programme, we were asked to devise a small-scale initiative that would improve quality of life for the locals. So we started by talking to them. They told us that traffic congestion was their biggest concern. The narrow streets are often clogged with both moving and parked cars.

Our moveable street bench doubles as a barrier to prevent parking and a place to sit, or to lock up bicycles. A robust, low-cost piece of design, it addresses the twin problems of traffic congestion and lack of street furniture. It's simple. It's cost effective. And it shows that small things can make a big difference.

Project name: Park/Park
Designed for: Dashilar Platform

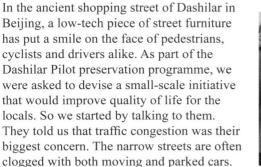

Birth of a megacity

Shanghai 1987
Completion of our first project

Our work in Shanghai: the first thirty years (1984-2014), and into the future

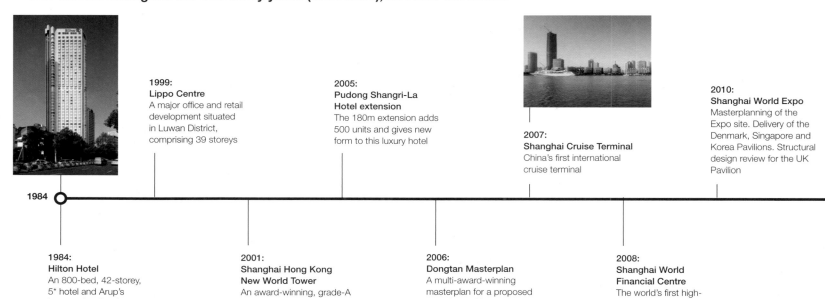

1999:
Lippo Centre
A major office and retail development situated in Luwan District, comprising 39 storeys

2005:
Pudong Shangri-La Hotel extension
The 180m extension adds 500 units and gives new form to this luxury hotel

2007:
Shanghai Cruise Terminal
China's first international cruise terminal

2010:
Shanghai World Expo
Masterplanning of the Expo site. Delivery of the Denmark, Singapore and Korea Pavilions. Structural design review for the UK Pavilion

1984

1984:
Hilton Hotel
An 800-bed, 42-storey, 5* hotel and Arup's inaugural project in China, completed 1987

2001:
Shanghai Hong Kong New World Tower
An award-winning, grade-A office block and cultural hub after its 'art mall' rebranding

2006:
Dongtan Masterplan
A multi-award-winning masterplan for a proposed eco-city on Chongming Island

2008:
Shanghai World Financial Centre
The world's first high-rise to feature shuttle lifts for fire evacuation

Shanghai 2013
The city that keeps on growing

2013:
Hongqiao Tiandi
This eco-efficient economic hub has four office towers and a hotel

2013:
Jing'an Kerry Centre
The three-towered luxury mall is a retail and gourmet hub

2014:
Shanghai International Commerce Centre
A landmark commercial complex atop a metro interchange

2016:
Shanghai Expo UBPA redevelopment
A pedestrianised, eco-friendly development built on the former Expo site

2022:
TOD Town, Shanghai
The redevelopment and expansion of the town's station into a multi-transport hub with 17 buildings

2025

2011:
Shanghai Oriental Sports Centre
A unique complex with indoor and outdoor swimming pools

2014:
White Magnolia Plaza
A 320m curved high-rise and two hotel towers

2015:
Shanghai Tower
The world's second tallest building at 632m

2017:
Shanghai Shipyards
The redevelopment of this historical area, with plans for hotels, offices, entertainment and homes

"People say a major change takes place every three years, but, in Shanghai, you see a major change every three months. The pace of the city gets faster and faster."

Dr Zhang, doctor of Chinese medicine, specialising in acupuncture

Some cities don't just evolve; they are transformed. Nowhere is this better shown than in Shanghai. Through unprecedented growth over three decades, it has become a megacity. Its changing skyline tells the story of its metamorphosis into a global economic and cultural powerhouse.

We have been part of this transformational journey since the 1980s, when we created the first of the city's skyscrapers: the 42-floor Hilton Hotel. Back then, change was characterised by significant new buildings.

Today, the city is highly populated and has expanded well beyond its former boundaries. The creative reuse of land is one of our priorities.

>

"The increase in the population has resulted in a higher density in the city centre. Shanghai is full of creativity and ideas. I feel I'm brainstorming constantly."

Yifei, architect

"The site of the Shanghai Expo used to be a very rough area, so rough that no one would bother to come out here. But the Expo changed the face of the whole place."

Kay, account executive with an advertising agency

> "Many different modern buildings and spaces coexist with the old architecture. Shanghai really does have its own character."

Pei Er Chen, works in the textile industry

This is shown in the redevelopment of the 2010 Shanghai World Expo site, which lies on the west bank of the Huangpu River. We created a masterplan and are overseeing the reuse of this area, which was once used for industrial workshops. Construction is under way to implement our low-carbon, eco-friendly plan, which includes a business, leisure and exhibition centre. This will be the Expo Urban Best Practice Area (UBPA). It is already held up as a shining example of what is possible in low-carbon development in China.

Another scheme that shows the creative reuse of land is TOD (transport-orientated development) Town Shanghai in Xinzhuang. We recognised the potential to do more with the existing metro station, which will become a multi-transport hub. We are also developing a mixed-use development above this. It is the first existing station to have residential, retail and office space all in the same place.

Hongqiao Tiandi is another transport hub we've worked on. Shanghai has grown so much that this airport, previously some 14km to the west, is now part of the city. The airport has existing local metro and

>

"My father was a sailor and my mother used to take me to the shipyard to listen to the ships' horns. Now that he is retired, we sometimes take a nostalgic walk there."

Rafael, jewellery designer with LVMH

ground transport links, as well as rail links to other Chinese cities. This means it's ideally positioned for development. The new centre, the Starship, will be home to four office towers, a hotel, shopping malls and an exhibition centre.

At Shanghai Shipyards, we are engineering several new buildings and renovating an existing 1970s ship factory. This redevelopment will be an extension of the existing financial centre at Lujiazui District in Pudong. It will provide hotels, offices, entertainment complexes and commercial and residential property.

We are unlocking new opportunities for economic growth in an already busy city and, in the process, helping to create a better experience for those who live and work here. However, the transformation of Shanghai is far from over. In a country that prides itself on putting infrastructure in place to attract people, it is at the forefront of the rapid urbanisation expected throughout China. This model of reuse and expansion is effective, ongoing and sure to be followed elsewhere.

"In 1978, the People's Bank was the only bank in all of China. Our office was on the Bund, number 23, and it was the best building in Shanghai at the time."

Mrs Zhang, retired bank manager

Connections for growth

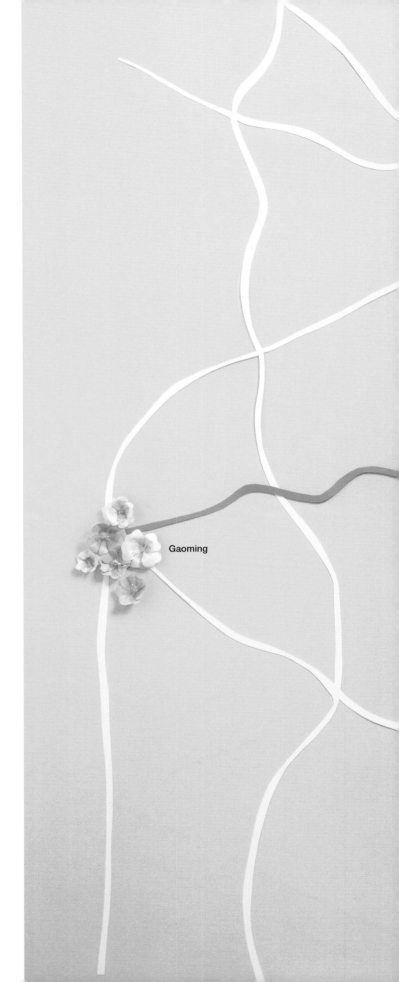

Gaoming

Trains don't just move people. They change the economies of cities. In Foshan, Guangdong, China, we harnessed this power by adjusting the route of a new metro line to prioritise station locations that will drive growth. After studying existing plans for the route, we focused on positioning stations in neighbourhoods where development opportunities lay, supporting the business case for the privately funded network.

It's a sustainable model. Commercial and residential buildings, shared social spaces and other infrastructure can be built in stages. This means costs can be recouped during the construction and operation of the new metro lines.

Best of all, when it is finished, local communities will enjoy increased connectivity and long-term socioeconomic benefits from the regeneration of the area.

Project name: TOD, planning design and financing of Foshan Metro Line 2 and 3
Designed for: Foshan Municipal Government; Planning Bureau Foshan Metro
Designed with: Ronald Lu & Partners

Foshan West station

Railway station

Guicheng

TV Tower

Shiwan

Kuiqi Road

Wanhua

Flower Market

Dongping

Guangzhou
South station

Beijiao

Daliang

Desheng

Ronggui

Credits

Park/Park, p123
Small design, big impact
Photography: courtesy of Arup

Passenger Railcar Blast Vulnerability, p65
Safety by design
Photography: Afton Almaraz / Getty Images

Regent Street Freight Reduction Scheme, p26
Delivering a new shopping experience
Photography: Jorg Greuel / Getty Images

The Reid Building, p102
Best of both worlds
Illustration: Courtesy of Steven Holl Architects;
photography: McAteer Photograph / courtesy of Arup;
Johanna Ward / Wardour

Rijksmuseum, Amsterdam, p42
That's how the light gets in
Photography: John Lewis Marshall / courtesy of Arup

Route 7 electric bus demonstration programme, p52
Keeping the wheels turning
Illustration: Jamie Jones / MP Arts

Sensing City, p40
A smart city in action
Illustration: Kyle Bean; photography: Mitch Payne

Singapore Sports Hub, p100
Sporting showcase
Photography: © Darren Soh / courtesy of Arup

Sky Believe in Better Building, p49
Wood can be tall... and sustainable
Illustration: Kyle Bean; photography: Johanna Ward /
Wardour

**Support to the Office of Housing Recovery
Operations, p90**
Retrofitting resilience
Illustration: Emma Shoard

Taoyuan Aerotropolis, p62
Flying high
Photography: iStockphoto

Teachers Village, Newark, p18
A sustainable education
Illustration: SoMa-Halsey

The High Roller, p108
Evolution for revolution
Photography: courtesy of Arup

**TOD, planning design and financing of Foshan Metro
Line 2 and 3, p134**
Connections for growth
Illustration: Morning Sets

Torre Reforma, p92
To build high, build low
Illustration: Wardour

Tottenham Regeneration Strategy, p76
A spur for change
Photography: Shutterstock; Johanna Ward / Wardour

Transbay Transit Center, p74
Managing vibrations
Photography: Lee George Hacker / Pixeleyes Photography

Tshwane Inner City Regeneration Project, p116
Capital gains
Photography: courtesy of Arup

UK Central, p122
A train that gives heart
Illustration: Tovelisa; map data: © OS OpenData Ordnance
Survey, Crown Copyright and Database rights 2014;
contains public sector information licensed under the Open
Government Licence V.3.0

White Collar Factory, p66
The future works
Photography: Matt Chisnall / courtesy of Arup

Wood is good, p47
Photography: iStockphoto

**Working Together: Global Aggregation of City Climate
Commitments, p82**
Shining example
Photography: Science Photo Library

Our work in Shanghai, p124
Birth of a megacity
Photography: Tom Bonaventure / Getty Images; Stringer /
Reuters; Carlos Barria / Reuters; © Kingkay Architectural
Photography; © CSSC Complex Property Co Ltd / courtesy
of Arup; Raphael Olivier

Commentaries

Thomas Heatherwick, p96
British heritage, global reach
Photography: Elena Heatherwick

Clover Moore, p68
Designing tomorrow's city
Photography: Greg Piper

Edgar Pieterse, p38
Towards a more just city
Photography: Red Petal

Judith Rodin, p80
Building resilient cities
Photograph supplied by Judith Rodin

Additional project credits

Adelaide Oval Redevelopment, p94
Services consultants: AECOM; Aurecon
Project managers: Mott MacDonald

Cities Alive, p13
Rethinking green infrastructure, Arup

Cityringen, Denmark, p29
Specialist consultant: Atkins; Ramboll Joint Venture

**Development Sustainability Principles framework and
ecology masterplan, p24**
Regent Street Direct; BNP Paribas

Rijksmuseum, Amsterdam, p42
Van Hoogevest Architects;
Jean-Michel Wilmotte; Vantlengten; HNR VOF; DGMR

**Inditex Fire Emergency Plans; Inditex Structural
Surveys; Accord Review of Standards; Accord
Structural Surveys; ILO Quality Assurance for Safety
Inspections, p70**
Statistics source: Accord on Fire and Building Safety
in Bangladesh

The Arup Design Book is produced and published
for Arup by Wardour

For Arup
Arup Design Book Publishing Board
Malcolm Smith, Tristram Carfrae, Mark Bidgood

David Boreham, Project Director
Victoria Wootton, Project Manager

For Wardour
The core team was led by Claire Oldfield, who also took
the editorial lead, and Ben Barrett, who took the creative
lead. The team included: art editor Lynn Jones, picture
editor/photographer Johanna Ward, project managers
Georgina Beach and Ella Kilgarriff.

Thanks to the writers, editors, researchers and artworkers
who worked alongside the core team and with the wider
production team – there are too many to mention.

Wardour, Drury House, 34–43 Russell Street,
London WC2B 5HA, United Kingdom
+44 (0)20 7010 0999
www.wardour.co.uk

'wardour '

Arup Design Book is printed
by Hampton Printing Limited, Bristol
on FSC certified material.

FSC
www.fsc.org
MIX
Paper from
responsible sources
FSC® C016102

Arup Design Book
50 city stories explored
ISBN no: 978-0-9538239-5-6